CW00548323

A SYMBOL FOR THE FESTIVAL
Abram Games and the Festival of Britain

Cover artwork for *Design* magazine,
Number 7, Festival of Britain issue, July 1949

A SYMBOL FOR THE FESTIVAL
Abram Games and the Festival of Britain

Naomi Games

CAPITAL HISTORY

For my dearest Theo, with love

ACKNOWLEDGEMENTS
Special thanks for the invaluable support and humour of my son, Theo and my siblings Daniel, Sophie and with love for our dearest parents, Abram and Marianne.

Much appreciation goes to Jim Whiting, a patient and tolerant publisher and editor and to Lucy Frontani. A big thank you also to Chris Mees and Eric Levene for endless souvenirs and support for the archives.

This book could not have been written without the generous help of the following: Douglas Muir; the British Postal Museum and Archives, Hugh Alexander; the National Archives UK, Zoe Hendon; Museum of Domestic Design and Architecture, London, Caterina Benincasa, Mona Gordon, née Caller, Henrietta Goodden, Michael Thatcher, Susan Wright, Fred Peskett, the family of George Simner, the Festival of Britain Society, Michael and Lyn Hymers, Brian Powney, Dinah Wood, Rebecca Pearson, Graham Ward, Martin Andrews, University of Reading and Kenzo Ejiri.

Thanks to all the untraceable Festival photographers and cartoonists of 1951.

Title page: Abram at home, 1951. Marianne embroidered the star cushion on the chair. The Festival paper dancers on the top of the bookshelf were designed by George Adams-Teltscher.

Back cover: Abram Games at Ann Creed Books, London, 1991

Endpapers: Festival wrapping paper, designer unknown

PICTURE CREDITS
Pages 32, 33, 36, the British Postal Museum and Archives.
Pages 8, 13, 14, 24, 25, 39, 41–45, 51, 57, 68, 77, the National Archives UK.
Page 9 Getty Images
Page 20, the American Museum in Britain, Bath.
Page 60, Transport for London.
Page 78, the 'British Cartoon Archive, University of Kent'.
Page 81, 'Courtesy of Cardiff Libraries and Information Service'.

Estate of Abram Games can be contacted at:
n.games1@virginmedia.com
www.abramgames.com

ISBN 978-1-85414-345-7

Published by
Capital History Publishing
www.capitalhistory.com

Printed by
1010 Printing International Ltd

CONTENTS

1951
THIS IS
FESTIVAL YEAR
This is 1951, the year of Britain's great Festival. What does it mean? It means that Britain is on show to the world, and that includes everything in and of Britain. The miracles of British science . . . and the vigour and skill of British sport. British industry in all its busy variety . . . and the deeply-felt faith of British churches. The glory of British music . . . and the lovely British countryside and its people. The whole country puts its best face forward to the world–*and to itself*.
OVER hard years and happy ones, through stirring times that settled down to become history, we have built up—sometimes from scratch again—the things that make the way we live. It was hard work, and there'll be more of it, but it gives us something well worth having. And now, in 1951, the world is coming to see what we've done, what we're going to do and what we're made of—the sort of people we are, the sort of things we like and do well. People are going to find the real interest in every part of Britain. There'll be something for everyone to see—and each one of us has a chance to join in. Indeed, Their Majesties The King and The Queen, Patrons of the Festival, have expressed the hope that every family will share in it. Exciting events are being arranged all over the country, as well as giant exhibitions and arts festivals in main centres. Putting the whole country on show for the first time is a big job; but all of us together can show that Britain is still something well worth seeing—and that we still know how to enjoy ourselves!
FESTIVAL OF BRITAIN
Britain at home to the world
May 3—September 30

INTRODUCTION

'There are two ways of thinking of the Festival. One would be to look upon it merely as a welcome, if temporary, release from the drab days of austerity and a restricted life. The better method is to think of 1951 as something more than just an end in itself. Besides the festivities, it can be an opportunity to lay the foundations of many good and better things to come.' Sir George Aylwen, Lord Mayor of London, 1951

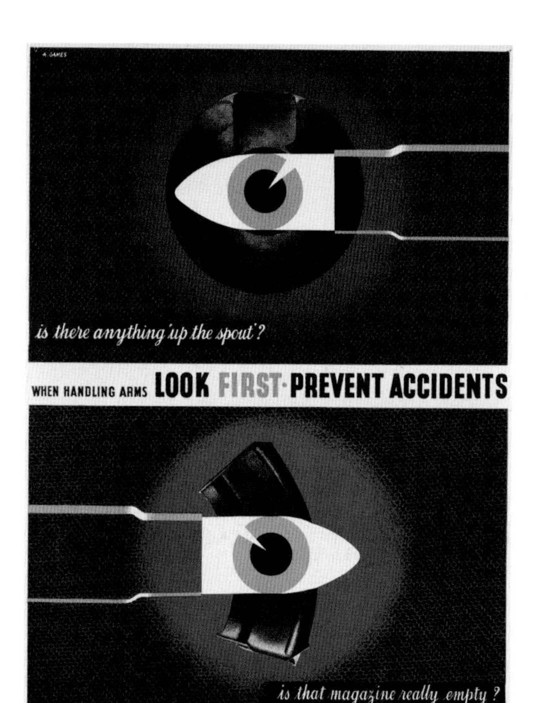

War Office poster, 1942

Whitehall, London SW1
1st April 1946

To whom it may concern:

Captain A. Games has served in the Public Relations Directorate of the War Office from June 1941, until March 1946.

During that period he designed many very successful posters, which were most useful in connection with Army Public Relations work. In this field Captain Games had a difficult and diverse set of subjects for treatment, which ranged from the design of posters directed to instilling a sense of security or impressing the need for hygiene to poster publicity work in support of recruiting campaigns. His work had to be subtly persuasive or directly "propagandist" – but it was always effective, compelling, and of outstanding quality.

I venture to regard him as quite exceptionally qualified in his art, and his services to the Army were very valuable.

PH O'Donnell

Major General
Director of Public Relations

War Office poster, 1943

Armed with this testimonial, de-mobbed Captain Abram Games, creator of one hundred war posters and holder of the unique title of 'Official War Poster Artist', felt well qualified to set up as a freelance designer. Although he had designed many flow charts, maps, book covers, murals and advertisements, it was his poster work that was to become recognised by the British public.

Commissions trickled into his Surbiton studio from his pre-war clients; the Royal Society for the Prevention of Accidents, the General Post Office and London Transport. British European Airways and the British Industries Fair requested posters too. But he was most fulfilled when accepting work from the British Empire Campaign, the United Nations, the Central British Fund and Palestine's Ambulance Corps, as he primarily wanted to design posters for social and educational purposes rather than carry out purely commercial work.

He believed that after the war, it would be the poster that would offer the best means of liaison between government and the people during reconstruction. Abram was establishing himself as an independent practitioner and from 1946 for the next seven years, was to teach Graphic Design one day a week at the Royal College of Art in London.

Having initiated the organization of the 1851 Great Exhibition, in 1943 the Royal Society for the Encouragement of Arts, Manufacturers and Commerce, suggested marking its centenary. Two years later, *News Chronicle* editor Gerald Barry was inspired to write a letter in his paper to Sir Stafford Cripps, President of the Board of

RoSPA poster, 1946

United Nations Day poster, 1948

BEA, Olympic Games poster, 1947

BEA to BIF poster, 1948

Trade. Barry suggested that the nation should hold a cultural exhibition, celebrating the centenary of the Great Exhibition. This would also be an opportunity to internationally promote and advertise post war Britain's design and manufacturing skills. Cripps was keen on the idea of regular British trade fairs, but thought that it might be impossible to stage an 'International Exhibition' in London involving large scale demands of labour and materials without affecting the progress of urgent post war reconstruction. A government committee chaired by Lord Ramsden, was set up to consider the proposal.

On 5th December 1947, Herbert Morrison, deputy Prime Minister of Clement Attlee's Labour government and Leader of the House of Commons, announced the Government would hold a 'Festival of Britain' in 1951. It would be 'a national display illustrating the British contribution to civilization, past, present and future, in the arts, in science and technology, and in industrial design.'

This page:
Two views of parts of the South Bank site prior to the Festival, 1948/9

Opposite:
The Dome of Discovery in construction, 1950

The Festival was to be a party to which not only London, but also the whole of austerity Britain would be invited. The King said every family in the land should share it. It was to be a 'tonic to the nation' – a nation which was still suffering from rationing and post-war exhaustion. This celebration was to be organized and financed by the state.

Much to Cripps's chagrin, plans for an international trade fair were abandoned due to financial and political restraints. The responsibility for the Festival was passed to Morrison, who was also the Lord President of the Council. The Great Exhibition Centenary Committee made up of various interested departments was appointed to create the Festival of Britain.

Under the direction of Sir Gerald Barry, a distinguished team of young architects, designers, engineers, scientists and artists would be employed to create a Festival site in London and organize a travelling exhibition for the provinces. Unbeknown to them, this would give those involved the unique opportunity to make their mark on their professions.

THE FESTIVAL SYMBOL

In the last week of May 1948, Abram, his pregnant wife Marianne and their first child, Daniel, moved to a house with a studio in Golders Green, north west London. On 9th June he received a letter from Gerald Barry, Director-General of the Festival of Britain. Abram would have no idea of the effect this was to have on his career.

Dear Mr Games,

The Executive Committee is seeking a design for a symbol for the Festival of Britain now being planned to mark the centenary of the Great Exhibition of 1851.

You have been selected to be invited to take part in a strictly limited competition, full particulars of which are attached, and I should be obliged if you would let me know, by not later than June 21, whether or not you are able to participate.

Not more than twelve designers are being approached; by limiting this contest in this way it is thought that we shall be more likely to achieve a design of vitality and distinction.

The conditions have been kept to a bare minimum and are intended for guidance only. You will, I am sure, applaud the decision not to hamper the designer by imposing upon him a rigid framework into which the design must be pressed.

What form the design takes is left to the designer's own taste and judgment. It is, however stressed, perhaps needlessly, that the symbol must be simple in form, have popular appeal, and be readily recognizable.

Abram, now thirty-four years old, studied the attached brief with interest. This would be a challenge he could not resist.

SYMBOL FOR THE FESTIVAL OF BRITAIN 1951

1. *A symbol is required for the Festival of Britain to be held in the summer of 1951. It is intended that it shall be used in connection with all official activities of the Festival, and as a mark of recognition awarded by the Festival Authorities to all approved non-official activities.*
2. *The symbol must be simple in design, recognizable at a glance, and fully effective on a scale suitable for letter-headings, tickets, posters and lapel badges as well as on an architectural scale. It must also be equally effective in either black and white or full colour.*
3. *The purpose of the Festival is to present to the world, in exhibitions and other ways, the British contribution to civilization, past and present, and future, in the Arts, in Science and Technology, in Architecture and Building Research, and in Industrial Design.*
4. *The principal activities will be –*

a. *Large-scale Festivals covering music, drama and art in all parts of the United Kingdom.*
b. *A Festival version of the British Industries Fair.*
c. *A large-scale combined exhibition embracing industrial design, the arts, science and architecture.*
d. *A large-scale exhibition of science and technology.*
e. *An exhibition covering architecture, town planning, and building research.*

Evacuation Scheme window card, 1939

f. *A travelling exhibition will tour the country.*
5. *As the Festival marks the centenary of the Great Exhibition of 1851 it is suggested you that you should bear in mind the possible advantages of incorporating the date of "1951".*
6. *You are invited to submit designs in black and white, in full colour and in two sizes (a) letterhead size (b) poster size. Designs should be sent to the Director-General, Festival of Britain 1951, 2, Savoy Court, Strand, London, WC2 no later than 15th September 1948. For this work a fee of Fifty Guineas is offered. Should your design be accepted you will be commissioned to provide finished drawings, the copyright of which will be vested in the Controller, HMSO, for a fee of Two Hundred and Fifty Guineas. The successful designer will be expected to carry out reasonable alterations, if required, without additional fee.*
7. *The number of designers invited to take part is limited to 12.*
8. *From the designs submitted a preliminary selection will be made by the Director-General and the Executive Committee; the final choice will be the unalterable decision of the Council of the Festival of Britain, 1951.*
9. *The Assessors retain the right to withhold the fee in any case where it is considered that the designer has made no genuine effort to meet the requirements laid down.*

Point two of the brief suited Abram's personal philosophy of 'maximum meaning, minimum means'. However, having primarily produced posters, Abram was not yet experienced in the design of emblems. In 1939 he had designed a window card for the National Evacuation Scheme, then a cap badge for the Royal Armoured Corps in 1942, and an emblem for Jewish Child's Day in 1944. But it was not until he considered his first stamp design for the 1948 Olympic Games in 1947 he fully appreciated that, in a work which was to be reproduced so small in scale, one of the most difficult things to achieve was impact. He would however, accomplish this through simplicity. In fact the more obstacles he had to conquer, the more he relished the challenge and the more disciplined a designer he was to become. He was unfazed by working in monochrome, having been accustomed to printing restrictions during the war. He believed single colour must be 'massed in terms of psychological and dramatic order' and that the drawing itself must take over the function of colour. Proportion, balance, rhythm and space, must all be considered. Abram must have relished the idea of being given a 'free hand'. He was used to working without interference from the client and since the age of twenty-two, when he had been sacked by Askew Younge's commercial art studio for 'independent views', vowed never to take orders from anyone ever again, except from his army superiors.

In July 1948 Abram told the magazine *Art & Industry*, "The first requirement of a designer is that he should fully understand the problem he is faced with. I make it a rule to acquaint myself with every possible aspect and gain as much information as is relevant to the job. Sometimes a brief talk, literature on the subject or one's own common sense and experience make this a simple matter. More often there are subjects, which require long and careful research work. At this stage, the designer as a specialist himself should always welcome the advice of specialists in other fields. I have often found that a visit to a works opens up new avenues of thought and experience and serves to keep me on the right track. Knowledge of the job, then, is of the first importance."

The Director of the Council of Industrial Design, Gordon Russell, and his committee unanimously agreed to keep the conditions of designing the symbol to a bare minimum. They suggested more time be given to the designers, with three months being deemed sufficient. Their colleagues at the Society of Industrial Artists were opposed in principle to limited competitions since they preferred to give lesser-known designers a chance to enter. They however acknowledged that, with an open competition, top designers would be reluctant to participate, but might do so if the cause was of national importance. The committee advised that a fee of sixty guineas for each finished rough should be offered to all entrants and the winner's total fee should be no less than 300 guineas. They questioned whether it should be policy to select only designers of British origin. The CoID suggested that Milner Gray, John Armstrong, Richard Guyatt, Robin Day and Abram Games should be asked to enter and then added that if any of these dropped out, Edward Bawden and Jesse Collins should be contacted.

In fact the following eleven designers received the same brief as Abram:

John Armstrong (1893–1973) was a British painter and designer. He was an Official War Artist during World War Two and designed a mural for the Festival of Britain.

Edward Bawden (1903–1989) was a British painter, printmaker, illustrator and designer. Like Armstrong, he was an Official War Artist during the war and worked on the Lion and Unicorn Pavilion for the Festival of Britain.

Milner Connorton Gray (1899–1997), a British designer, worked for the Ministry of Information during the war and was a founder of the Society of Industrial Artists and Designers and the Design Research Unit. He was responsible for the signage of the Festival of Britain.

Frederic Henri Kay Henrion (1914–1990), designer, was born in Germany and became a British national in 1946. He worked for the Ministry of Information during World War Two and was the designer of the Festival of Britain's Country Pavilion on the South Bank.

Theyre Lee-Elliott (1903–1988) was British born and designed posters for the Ministry of Labour during the war. He is best known as the designer of the 'Speedbird' emblem for Imperial Airways.

Robin Day (1915–2010), British born, was a graphic and furniture designer. Whilst in the Royal Air Force during the war, he designed posters for the Air Ministry. In 1951, he designed the furniture for the new Royal Festival Hall and for two rooms in the Festival of Britain's House and Gardens Pavilion.

Richard Guyatt (1914–2007), designer, was born in Spain. He helped reform the Royal College of Art, working there for thirty-four years, first as professor, then as Pro-Rector, then Rector. During the war he served as Regional Camouflage Officer for Scotland for the Ministry of Homeland Security. He co-designed the Lion and Unicorn pavilion for the Festival and was responsible for the display on British Law and the design of flock wallpaper.

Lynton Lamb (1907–1977), Indian born and educated in Britain, was a painter, illustrator, lithographer, wood engraver and designer. Like Guyatt, he worked as a camouflage artist during the war. One of his paintings was exhibited at the Festival of Britain.

Tom Eckersley (1914–1996) was a British poster designer and illustrator. During World War Two he was a cartographer for the Royal Air Force and designed posters for the Air Ministry and the Ministry of Information. He also designed many posters at this time for the Royal Society for the Prevention of Accidents. He was Head of Graphic Design at the London College of Printing for twenty years.

Alan Reynolds Stone (1909–79) was a British wood engraver, stone letter carver, typographer, illustrator and painter. During World War Two he served in the photo interpretation division of the Royal Air Force. He designed a Festival seal for the Festival of Britain.

Peter Ray (1917–1990) was a British typographer, graphic and exhibition designer. He worked in the design team of the Ministry of Information during World War Two and was responsible for the Festival of Britain Health and Welfare Pavilion.

Robin Day's Festival symbol competition entries

Milner Gray

Richard Guyatt

Lynton Lamb

Tom Eckersley

Theyre Lee-Elliot

John Armstrong

FHK Henrion

Alan Reynolds Stone

Designer unknown

Peter Ray

Many of these artists began their careers designing posters for Shell-Mex and were commissioned by its astute Art Director, Jack Beddington. Although their Festival symbols were not chosen, with the exception of Lee-Elliot, Eckersley and Lamb, they would make a significant contribution to the design of the Festival of Britain.

Happy to be amongst these elite designers, most of whom he knew well, the practitioner of the visual *double-entendre* worked on the symbol at home whilst builders were demolishing his kitchen. His studio, however, remained as immaculate as ever. After gestating on a design, Abram dedicated himself to its success. No idea was sacrosanct. With his treasured War Office dustbin at his side, he was never afraid to discard his progressive sketches.

Perched on a tall stool at his homemade desk overlooking the garden, he attacked the layout pad armed with a cigarette, sharpened blue pencil and gouache paint. He concentrated hard and worked quickly. Amongst his abundant loose change Abram readily found an iconic British symbol on a penny in his pocket. From the start, Britannia was to epitomize the spirit of the nation and the four cardinal points were to represent the whole of Britain. The Union Jack and arrows were considered too, but by the last sheet of sketches, he denoted patriotism by introducing the red, white and blue of the flag without borrowing its other elements.

On the first sheet of paper, the head faces to the right, as it does on the coin, but like his other wartime designs, he soon had her facing optimistically to the left. Abram was a socialist

British penny, 1949

and a Labour government was in power after all! He initially placed the compass points within Britannia's head and helmet, but soon abandoned this design when he realised his initial ideas were perhaps too martial; not surprisingly, as he had been designing posters for war for five years. On the next two sheets of layout paper, the original idea is explored and manipulated. The Festival brief was never out of sight. He reflected that the design should not be overpowering, but positive and constructive, whilst embodying the Festival spirit. It must combine impact with significance, be memorable, and there should be more to discover when seeing it repeatedly. In the same instance it had to be instantly recognisable and say not only 'Festival', but also 'Britain'. He understood the importance of the symbol's versatility, which had to serve as a good marketing tool, be capable of reduction to postage stamp size, and yet translate into both two and three dimensions, for publicity and architectural use. The elements should be brought together into a single element and tied by logic and form. His designs were very much a matter of internal reflection and subconscious thought allied with experience. He believed a sense of purpose should pervade every design so that it reached in and proclaimed its individuality. Without it, he considered a design remained merely decoration. In every one of his designs the intricacies of engineering were so well concealed that the final design emerged as ridiculously simple and inevitable. Abram often placed a sketchy grid over his final work to prove that his instinctive sense of geometry was functioning to his satisfaction. He did not expect the symbolism of his design to be immediately obvious to people, nor did he expect everyone to like it at first. If whatever he designed was merely *noticed*, and not ignored, he was satisfied.

"I usually have the brief in my head for a while before putting pencil to paper. The final design gradually evolves from the many progressive drawings I make". He explained.

On the 9th September 1948, Abram was sent a letter to remind him of the deadline for the competition. He received a receipt for his submission 15th September. A consummate professional, he always met his deadlines even though this would often require working throughout many days and nights. As a family man working from a home where everyone was welcome at most times, he preferred the solitude of working at night as it was quiet and he would not be interrupted by children, visitors or telephone calls. Between the twelve designers, sixteen entries were submitted. Perhaps Edward Bawden didn't enter the competition, as there is no record of his entry in the National Archive in Kew, though the designer of one entry remains unidentified. Abram, as usual, only presented one design. A determined man, who had the courage of his convictions, he was forever confident in his work. He maintained that if the designer could not decide on the very best solution to a design brief, how could the client rely on him? Besides, the more alternatives shown, the less likely the client would like any of them. However, on this occasion he submitted various adaptations of his one design. He offered both one and eight inch high versions in black ink,

Left and right: Progressive drawings for the Festival of Britain symbol, 1948

2
1951
1951
759

Progressive drawings for the Festival of Britain symbol, 1948

and the same sizes of artwork in colour gouache, giving the larger version a background of graduated, grainy ochre (to emulate gold).
Metal-based inks, especially yellow, were still being rationed. By using the airbrush given to him by his father Joseph, a photographer, not only did he economize on paint but also gave depth to Britannia's helmet and face. He was skilled using his trusted airbrush, a tool used for photographic retouching and adding colour to bromide prints.

The National Archive holds a memo dated 25th September from the Festival of Britain headquarters in Savoy Court in the Strand, London. It was distributed to the members of the Festival Executive: General Lord Ismay, Gerald Barry, Leonard Crainford, Paul Wright, Edward Max Nicholson, David Stephens and Miss JH Lidderdale.

The Director-General said that co-opted advisers had, after seeing the submitted designs, concluded the following:

Philip James chose Lynton Lamb's design first as did Sir Francis Meynell who placed Guyatt's second. Ralph Tubbs felt that although no design had reached the standard sought, Lamb and Guyatt should be asked to submit alternative designs. Sir Kenneth Clark also gave advice.

After much discussion it was felt that the executive could

a. *Accept the design as it was.*
b. *Ask the chosen artist or artists to modify or improve his present design or submit another.*
c. *Discard all designs and invite the same or other artists to start again.*

By the third sheet, having decided on his final design, Abram pencilled an outline around it, as was his habit. With some insight into his future success, he kept most of his post-war progressives, including these for the Festival of Britain symbol.

All agreed the time factor would not allow second attempts, which might not even produce better results. After more discussion, Lynton Lamb's and Abram's were judged the most suitable. Lamb's symbol was considered cheerful and full of movement, capturing the Festival spirit with a festive air. It could also be adopted for architectural use. However it had the disadvantage that it did not convey the seriousness of the Festival and might not be capable of reduction in size or monochrome reproduction. Abram's entry was 'an admirable and strikingly effective design in conception and execution. It would catch the eye and be remembered'. Against it was 'its military connotation, its Gallic, rather than British mien, its severity and complete absence of gaiety or festive idea.'

After the symbol was exposed to the public, newspaper critics continued to suggest Abram's Britannia was not only 'war-like' but very much like the French 'Marianne' in style. The two designs were then considered for uses on stationery, publicity and architecture.

It was decided to invite Games and Lamb to meet the Director-General to discuss modifying their original submissions or redesign a new symbol. Abram must have received this news by telephone, as no written record exists of this request. Having been asked to make his design 'more festive', he sat in his studio, wondering how to set about it. Looking out onto the garden one blustery day, he caught sight of his wife Marianne (who wasn't French!) hanging the family's washing on the clothesline. Often inspired by her, he also 'hung out the washing' and placed a garland of red, white and blue bunting, around Britannia. To do this, he had to slightly raise the italic figures '1951'.

A great admirer of the American born Edward McKnight Kauffer (1890–1954), Abram would be the first to admit that he was subliminally influenced by his work. Although these 1942 comparisons are tenuous, there is some evidence of his being inspired by this giant of poster design.

Original black and white submission artwork for the Festival symbol competition, 1948

Colour submission sketch for the symbol

Marianne in the garden with Daniel and Sophie, 1948

On 16th November 1948, Gerald Barry wrote to Abram apologizing for the delay in choosing a winning design and assured him the Festival Council would meet on 14th December and come to a conclusion. Barry wrote again a month later to say the Festival Council had come to a unanimous decision; that Abram's was the winning design and far excelled the other submissions in impact and clarity. He was asked to keep this news quiet until an official announcement was made. This was to be Abram's first governmental commission since the end of the war.

However, there were still changes to be made. The committee expressed the view that the figures '1951' were not sufficiently legible from a distance and requested that he consider strengthening them but without 'upsetting the unity of the design'. They noted that the date on the lapel badge design he submitted at the same time was bolder in proportion; in fact it overlapped the bunting. Abram was not a man who compromised and seems to have ignored these comments.

In a confidential memo entitled 'Use of the Festival Symbol' and circulated to the Executive Committee on 3rd December 1948, it was suggested the winning symbol be publicized first at a local authority gathering. It should be free for all to use, with no restrictions attached to it. Using the symbol would be of benefit to all associating with the Festival. It would 'be a tangible means of getting over to everyone the importance of standards and quality in things used and things done.' Recommendation was made to inscribe plaques and medals with the symbol and awards for design and architecture were to be given by the Festival Organization. By using the emblem, there would be no doubt that

Original colour submission artwork, 1948

Final colour submission artwork, 1948

Regional Festivals would be associated with the Festival of Britain.

Abram's symbol would be used in connection with all the official activities of the Festival and would be awarded as a mark of recognition by the Festival Authorities to all approved activities. The symbol would be used in various ways – in posters, stationery, tickets, lapel badges and architectural and official street decoration. All the competing designers of the Festival symbol were invited to view each other's designs on 5th January 1949.

An official press release was issued from the Festival Press Office at 2 Savoy Court, London WC2, at 1200 hours on 8th June 1949:

"A symbol has been adopted by the Council of the Festival of Britain 1951. The winning design was chosen by the Festival Council from entries received in response to a limited competition among specially selected designers. The advice of the Council of Industrial Design and of the Arts Council of Great Britain was sought in drawing up the initial list of competing designers.

The symbol designed by Abram Games, FSIA (Fellow of the Society of Industrial Artists) shows the head of Britannia surmounting the star of the compass. The surrounding pennants strike an appropriate festive note: the full colours are red, white and blue, alternately patterned on a gold ground."

Possibly Abram used, but slightly adapted the serifed, shaded 'Figgins' Roman type to reflect the Great Exhibition of 1851. Although he did not regard Britannia as a war-like figure, but rather considered she epitomised the spirit of the nation, he rethought the 'war-like' helmet design, before reaching the final version, making it start and end less abruptly by giving it gentle feminine, curves. Britannia's lips were given the same treatment.

It went on to say that to ensure correct reproduction, master drawings were available from the Press Office for anyone wanting to use the symbol. Manufacturers were asked to contact the Council of Industrial Design. A black and white photographic print of the symbol and biographical notes on Abram, a Fellow of the Society of Industrial Design, were enclosed with the press release.

In February 1949, the CoID received a letter from a Mr B. Ferst asking if a Festival symbol design had been chosen. Being a manufacturer of 'fancy goods and jewellery', he was keen to start manufacturing Festival souvenirs. Although the winning design was still a secret, the Festival office gave him a hazy description of the chosen emblem. Mr Ferst, was indeed the first to produce a range of high quality 'Starferst' tie pins, medals, badges, brooches, necklaces and spoons but with little resemblance to Abram's design.

Premature news of the symbol was also leaked to the *Observer* on 27th February 1949. It carried a vague representation of the winning design and referred to Abram as Abraham. The article exclaimed, 'the idea of a blue faced Britannia sounds queer, but is not symbolic, merely part of the design.' Although 'Abraham' appears on his birth certificate, from an early age, he preferred to be known as 'Abram'. Having deleted the un-kosher 'ham', the Jewish Abram was incensed when much of the press referred to him incorrectly. This was to happen throughout his six-decade career. Had he known he was called 'Abraham' in his obituaries, he would have resolved to haunt Fleet Street!

Small rough sketch submitted by Abram. This was used as a template for an enamel lapel badge.

Artwork for the Festival uniform, arm badge

Abram referred to this as the 'bastardised Starferst' interpretation of his symbol

The Observer's rendition of the Festival symbol, 27th February, 1949

Key drawing and artwork for the Festival of Britain symbol, 1948

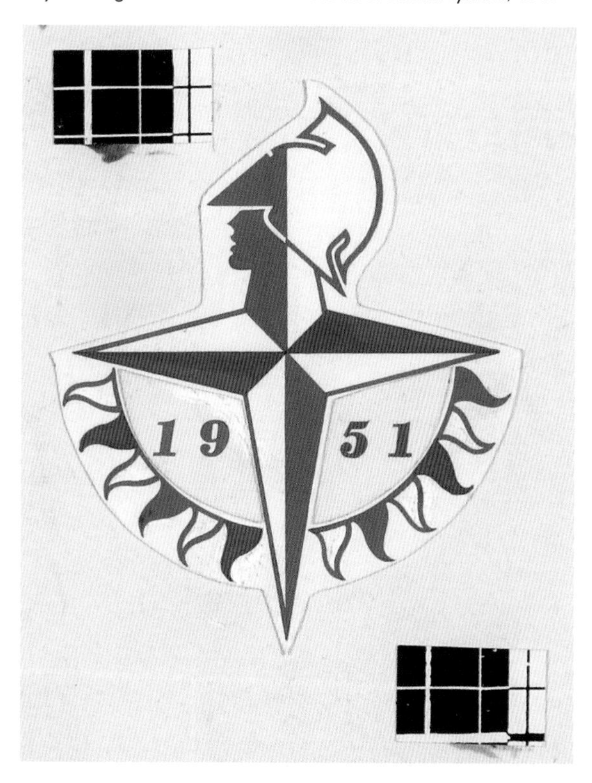

Letters were written to the *Observer*'s editor, and passed to an amused Abram to treasure. A Mr Kloegman wrote: 'I view with dismay the thought that this grotesque horror is what the world will be called upon to admire as a symbol of British achievement and culture. I feel bound to inquire if our commercial artists cannot produce something a little more inspiring than this third-form drawing of a befeathered and speared Sioux.'

In February 1949, *Art & Industry* published an article stating that the Festival of Britain was not an occasion for whipping up interest in freaks in the local museum, but a chance to take proper pride in people and things which have contributed or are contributing to the development of the life and soul of Britain. *Design*, a magazine issued by the Council of Industrial Design, commented in July 1949, 'Although there are no strings attached to use the symbol there is a patriotic obligation on each of us not to debase it by unworthy association, not to cheapen it for private gain and not to exploit it out of its context – for its context is clearly stated in the aims of the Festival itself: to show to the world Britain's contribution to civilization in the Arts, Sciences and Industrial Design.' It continued to declare that in the opinion of the CoID, if the symbol was to be an effective trade ambassador, every industry should uphold its value as a mark of British quality, craftsmanship and design. The CoID even suggested its long-term use as a 'Made in Britain' symbol.

Herbert Morrison was heard to point to the symbol and say " Not bad for a trade mark, eh?" Gerald Barry privately referred to her as

Festival label, designer unknown

'Madame Symbol'. As well as compliments like 'simple and striking' the emblem had its critics. Cartoonists lampooned it. Comments flowed easily, such as, 'the head looks uncomfortably impaled' and 'there ought to be a lion somewhere around'. *The Architect and Building News* thought it was just not good enough. *The Lancashire Daily Post* wrote 'Ever since we have had Britannia on our coinage she has looked to the right. Is it reading too much into the symbol to suggest that Britannia's left turn is a subtle compliment to Mr Herbert Morrison, the father of the Festival?'

Abram's record books show that on 14th June 1948, he received fifty guineas for the rough of the symbol. In January 1949, he was paid a further two hundred and fifty guineas for all versions of the final artwork. Much to his dismay, he could not maintain the copyright in this design. It was always his principle to hold the intellectual property of his work if possible. As the government commissioned the Festival symbol, it would become the copyright of the Crown, but with a proviso for unrestricted use to the public. It proved to be wonderfully adaptable and it was hoped it would soon be as well known as the Union Jack and the Olympic rings. Manufacturers were encouraged to produce official souvenirs featuring it, as it was a way to gain publicity. The CoID established a Festival Souvenir Committee, chaired by its director, Gordon Russell. They had monthly meetings, but to Abram's frustration his opinion was not sought. Predictably, manufacturers of souvenirs took the opportunity to profit from this national celebration. The Board of Trade expressed fears that overseas competitors might utilize it to impose non-British goods on the British consumer and warned that its unrestricted use would de-base the emblem. It allowed the import of foreign metal souvenirs under an open licence. The Supply Ministry was still banning the use of non-ferrous metals, making it harder to produce British official souvenirs. Unofficial Festival items flooded the market and many were made from the scrap alloy of wartime airplanes.

Years later, despite his achievement, Abram said of his ubiquitous Festival design, "Call it, anything you like, but never *logo*." His main agitation at the mention of this abbreviated and over-used word was its misuse; 'logos' is Greek for 'word' and a 'logotype' is a typographic representation of a company name. "I prefer symbol, emblem or trademark. They have been around since Ancient Egypt. I don't regard symbols with much affection. They don't have the same appeal as posters which I regard as my children." Abram's Britannia was the best-known symbol of the time and achieved wider application than any other for a national event. It would always be associated with the summer of 1951, a year which would be one of the most significant in his long career.

For the rest of his life, the 'Most Super of Festival Cranks', as Abram called himself, urged friends and family to hunt for Festival memorabilia. Whenever an item was discovered, his eyes lit up, a faint blush appeared on his cheeks and with a broad grin, and he would emit a delighted "Oooh!" He kept a cardboard box of Festival of Britain memorabilia in his studio.

The contents of the Festival of Britain time capsule, South Bank, London, 1951

Every so often he'd give in to our nagging and get it out for his excited children and we would rummage in the boxes for the treasure of balls, toys, horse-brasses and powder compacts. When our parents asked what we would like to do at the weekend, we would always request a trip to Battersea Park's Festival funfair. Whenever he took us to a concert on the South Bank, Abram would regale us with Festival memories and remind us that in October 1949, a first signed colour print of his Festival symbol was buried in a time capsule in the wall of the first floor of the Royal Festival Hall. Other items in the capsule were coins, a newspaper, London County Council documents, and a Festival hymn.

Always very proud to have made a contribution to this important event he kept a framed Festival emblem in pride of place in his studio until his death in 1996.

Opposite: Abram Games in his studio, 1951

THE FESTIVAL STAMP

In the spring of 1947, the Council of Industrial Design (CoID) proposed that the General Post Office should issue a range of special stamps to commemorate the forthcoming Festival of Britain and the centenary of the Great Exhibition. By February 1949, the Post Office Board accepted this idea and the concept of a set of commemorative special issue stamps, which were to be double the usual size and in horizontal format, was approved by King George V1 on 21st March.

The new Festival emblem was to be unveiled to the public at noon, on 8th June and although Sir Francis Meynell from the CoID was keen to use Abram's winning design on the stamps, the Director of Postal Services, Mr JE Yates, expressed concern. He failed to see how the Festival emblem could happily be juxtaposed with the King's head. However, after much discussion, Abram received an invitation to submit his design for a Festival of Britain stamp in the second week of June 1949. The following eleven artists, proposed by the CoID, were also invited to submit designs:

Mary Adshead, John R Barker, George R Bellew, Robin Day (he did not submit an entry), Edmund Dulac, Lewitt-Him (Jan Le Witt and George Him), Lynton Lamb, Enid Marx, Percy Metcalfe, Victor Reinganum and Hans Tisdall. Three artists from the printers Waterlows and one from Harrisons were also allowed to participate.

The first UK commemorative stamp (for the Wembley Exhibition) was issued in 1924 and so there had not been a stamp produced in 1851 to celebrate the Great Exhibition. Now the simple brief stated that the phrase 'Great Exhibition 1851-1951' must be included on the stamp. Artists were also advised that their designs must be pictorial rather than symbolic. The Post Office would consider submissions both with and without Abram's Festival symbol, which was, after all, free for all to use. It is certain Abram would not have been comfortable with any one else using his design, as plagiarism was abhorrent to him.

He had already won a successful stamp commission from the Post Office. The 1948 Olympic Games 3d violet 'speed' stamp had earned him the epithet 'Olympic Games' and he was delighted that his surname appeared on the stamp as designers were never allowed to sign their stamps. A year later, he designed a 2½d stamp, for the 75th Anniversary of the Universal Postal Union, 1874–1949. This was on a similar grid to the Festival stamp but was never published. Sadly, neither his 1952 low value and 1955 high value definitives nor 1953 Coronation stamps and 1958 Jersey Regionals were adopted by the Post Office either.

Unused UPU stamp design, 1949

Progressive sketches for the Festival of Britain stamp, designed in 1949

Unused Coronation stamp design by Abram, the intended colour is unknown, 1953

Progressive sketch for the 1948 Olympic Games stamp, designed in 1947

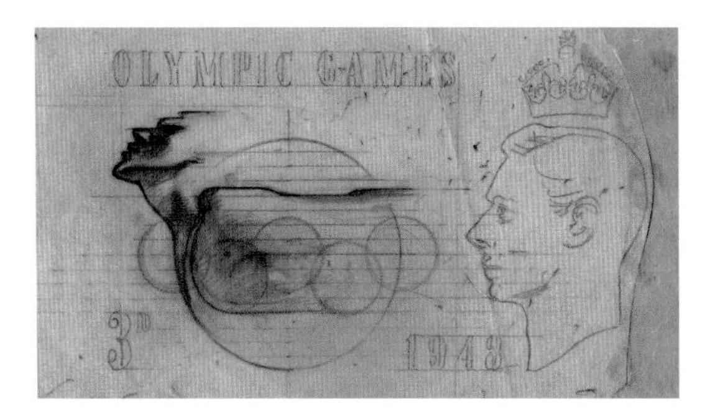

Sketch for the 1948 Olympic Games stamp, designed in 1947

1948 Olympic Games 3D stamp

Early in his career, realizing posters were mostly viewed from a distance, he maintained that if his final design could not to be read when an inch high it would fail as an advertisement. When devising a poster, he began by working through many sheets of small 'thumbnail' sketches, which he fastidiously pared down. Thus the design of a stamp would be second nature to Abram. Understanding how to reduce the whole meaning of the subject into a small area, he kept his design simple. Well aware of the limitations of stamp formats, the challenge was to incorporate the monarch's head and the required lettering whilst balancing the overall layout. Luckily for Abram, as Britain was the first country to use them, no British stamp was ever required to state the country of origin. But the head of the ruling monarch still had to occupy one third of the width of all British issues. In the mid-1960s, David Gentleman, a past Royal College of Art student of Abram's and subsequently a prolific stamp designer, successfully proposed that the monarch's head be depicted only as a small silhouette on all future pictorial stamp designs.

All stamps at this time were printed in a single colour by offset-litho or by intaglio photogravure. The latter used a photographic process to etch the design below the surface of copper cylinders. Later retouching was not advisable. A ruled screen was laid over the image, converting it into rows of cells or depressions of equal size but varying in depth; the solid areas containing more ink than the middle tones.

In 1953, the Israel Government's printer installed its first photogravure machine, for the printing of monochromatic stamps. It took them three years to realize that the process demanded a diverse approach to the design of stamps and the preparation of artwork. As Abram was considered experienced in the photogravure printing process after his work with the General Post Office, he received an invitation from the Ministry of Posts to conduct a course to teach Israel's stamp designers. In fact, Abram, was considered by Edmund Dulac to be 'one of the really up and coming men and one of the few who understood how to design for photogravure'. In the years from 1950 to 1973, Israel published six of the eight stamps Abram had designed for the new country.

Sir Gerald Barry and two other CoID representatives judged the Festival commemorative stamps in October 1949. Abram, predictably, only submitted one design. He must have considered himself fortunate his Festival symbol faced to the left so it did not conflict with the head of the King, which also faced to the left. After experimenting with several variations, Abram decisively placed scrolls inscribed with the commemorative years 1851 and 1951 on either side of his symbol.

A total of twenty-seven designs were submitted. One each by Edmund Dulac and George R Bellew and two by Victor Reinganum were short-listed. Abram's stamp was not selected but four other designers incorporated his symbol six times in their entries. It was decided in December that Dulac's design should become the 2½d stamp and Reinganum's the 3d. At this second meeting Abram's entry was reconsidered for the 3d stamp. It was also

Analysis of the stamp design

Sketch for the Great Exhibition centenary stamp

Submission artwork for the Great Exhibition centenary stamp

agreed to substitute 'Great Exhibition' with the text 'Festival of Britain'. At the end of December, Dulac's, Abram's, and two designs by Reinganum (which the Postmaster General did not favour) were sent to the chosen printers. Harrisons and Sons prepared stamp-sized bromides. On 10th February 1950, the three artists' revised designs were again considered. Dulac's design was preferred overall but now Abram's was the second choice. Ten days later Sir Allan Lascelles, the King's Private Secretary, was sent the three stamps with endorsements from the CoID. By 27th February, the King had approved Dulac's 2½d and Games's 3d stamps.

On 14th March 1950, Abram and Dulac[1] submitted their reworked drawings to Harrisons. It was agreed that Dulac's 'Commerce and Prosperity' design, depicting the head of Britannia and a cornucopia intertwined with a caduceus (the winged staff carried by the ancient god, Mercury), was to be printed in blue, whilst the Festival 3d stamp was to be violet. Abram was asked not only to alter the Britannia's helmet but also the King's crown and to make '3d' bolder. By July, as overseas postal rates increased, the denomination of the stamp had to change from 3d to 4d. The Post Office also decided to change Dulac's stamp to red and Abram's to ultramarine in line with the Universal Postal Union Convention.

---

1 Edmund Dulac, a book illustrator, set designer and portrait painter, was born in France in 1882. He designed several Free French Colonial and British stamps and banknotes. Settling in Britain in 1904, he was naturalized eight years later.

Submitted stamp design competition entries

Abram Games's design

Edmund Dulac's design

Mary Adshead's first design

Mary Adshead's first design (a variation)

Mary Adshead's second design

Mary Adshead's third design

Victor Reinganum's first design

Victor Reinganum's second design

Victor Reinganum's third design

Enid Marx's first design

Enid Marx's second design

Lewitt-Him's design

John R Barker's first design

John R Barker's second design

Stanley D Scott's (Harrisons and Sons Ltd), design

Hans Tisdall's first design

Hans Tisdall's second design

Hugo Fleury's (Waterlow and Sons Ltd), design

William HM McLaren's (Harrisons and Sons Ltd), first and second submitted designs

LD Fryer's (Waterlow and Sons Ltd), design

Percy Metcalfe's first design

Percy Metcalfe's second design

Lynton Lamb's first design

Lynton Lamb's second design

George Bellew's first design

George Bellew's second design

The Festival of Britain's 4d stamp

Abram and Dulac worked directly with Harrisons to produce colour essays. After many trial printings, both designers preferred the deeper rather than lighter colour shades for their stamps, which allowed an enhanced definition of their designs. Although Dulac was advised a deeper red would not satisfy the UPU Convention, his stamps were printed in the stronger magenta. However, the printer was concerned about maintaining the tone of a deeper blue throughout mass production and Abram's wishes went unheeded. He met the required tight deadline so that the stamps, printed in sheets of 120, could be produced in time. The final revisions were submitted to the King on 26th September 1950 and approved by him four days later. This was to be the last stamp issue of his reign. George VI died on 6th February 1952.

Dulac and Games received forty guineas for their submission designs (as did the other competing artists) and they both received a further 160 guineas on acceptance of their work.

Dulac and Abram's stamps cancelled with the Festival's hand stamp

Festival of Britain slogan die from a machine cancellation, 1951

Although doing all he could to achieve the best reproduction possible, Abram was ultimately unhappy with the final issue of his stamp. This was not unusual as he was a perfectionist and took great pride in his work. As was his practice, in October he asked to be sent a sample proof of the stamp. This colour essay had, however, been printed on a high quality, 100% Esparto paper, unlike the actual final stamp. When printing began in February 1951, he diligently visited the print works. Although praising the work of the Harrisons, he noted the head of the King was now much lighter than in the earlier proof he had approved. Harrisons had indeed 'improved' the definition of the monarch's head on the printing cylinders, with the consent of the General Post Office, who did not want the head overshadowed by the symbol. Printer and Post Office thought the change an improvement. However, Abram felt that the King was now unhappily competing with his Festival symbol and he was disappointed that he had not been consulted. This came as a shock to the bewildered Post Office; no other designer had ever complained about the printing of his stamps. But this was not to be Abram's first dispute with the GPO. From 1965 to 1967, he was a member of the Stamp Advisory Committee of the CoID and enlivened many a committee meeting with his strong, contentious, views. Unsurprisingly he did not successfully design any more British stamps, though he produced many award winning ones for Israel and a set for the channel island of Jersey.

At noon on 3rd May 1951, as King George V1 and Queen Elizabeth performed the opening

Stamp cancelling machine cancellation, for correspondence posted on the South Bank site, 1951

The City of Westminster issued eight 'On-my-Way' hexagonal stamps which sold for two shillings per sheet. Printed in various colours by Harrisons and Sons Ltd.

ceremony of the Festival of Britain at St Paul's Cathedral, the special commemorative stamps and nine other Festival stamps of differing high and low values in varying colours were issued. From midnight the night before, an eventual eight deep queue of collectors, dealers and the general public, were lining up outside Leicester Square and other United Kingdom Post Offices, eager to obtain the commemoratives. After twenty minutes, it was estimated that £1,000 worth of stamps had been sold. Extra staff had to be requisitioned for duty and there was still a queue at Post Office counters at two o'clock the next morning.

The Festival site on London's South Bank had its own Branch Office, with its own eight post boxes and a special postmark of Britannia. A vending machine on this site also issued parcel postage labels carrying the official symbol. JM Grice, who worked at the Architects Co-operative Partnership, designed the post office in York Road.

Throughout April, before the Festival of Britain opened, forty head post offices had issued an official Festival symbol postmark. Until 30th September, the day the Festival closed and when the commemoratives were withdrawn, envelopes could be hand-stamped or passed through a cancelling machine and franked with the symbol. Only post offices in the South East and the South Bank offered official stamp cancelling.

Although the General Post Office did not produce an official First Day Cover for the public, Harrisons produced an unknown quantity of 'souvenir cards' displaying the two stamps for private distribution. Patricia Chrome designed a ubiquitous souvenir envelope for the stamp dealer HE Wingfield, and the Philatelic Traders' Society and the British Philatelic Association issued the Boudicca envelope. The Reading Philatelic Society, Scottish Tourist Board, various dealers and businesses also produced their own envelopes. A total of 22,196,880 of Abram's 4d ultramarine stamps were sold. However, Dulac's stamp sold 260m.

Reactions to the official Commemorative stamps were mixed and, as always, kept Abram amused, so much so that he filed them in his own Festival album. The *Stamp Collector* of 5th May 1951 wrote 'the Festival is being brought to world's attention by the finest medium of propaganda ever designed – the postage stamp'. A letter to the editor of the *Continental Daily Mail*, Paris, 2nd July 1951, read 'Can anything be more horrible or in worse taste than the English Festival of Britain 4d stamp? Have we no artist in England capable of turning out something better than that?' The *Methodist Recorder* on the 10th May 1951 called Abram's stamp 'a complicated design with the shadowy head of Britannia and points of the compass surrounded by flags, which would seem unnecessarily intricate for popular use'. The *Nottingham Evening Post*, 3rd May 1951, announced that one philatelist stated 'They are just as bad as usual and lack imagination and attractiveness'. 'The 4d value, although an uninteresting design, is good compared with the 2½d.' said a letter in the *Times*, 8th May 1951. *Gibbons Stamp Monthly* 1st June 1951 stated that 'neither of the designs provides the slightest inspiration'.

The Festival Branch Post Office on the South Bank site, 1951

This pillar box, one of eight, stood in front of the Power and Production pavilion on the South Bank site, 1951

Abram was nevertheless the first stamp designer in the United Kingdom who was privileged to be able to include a symbol of his own design in one of his own stamps. On 3rd May 1951, he sent his parents a letter, enclosing the blue Festival 4d.

My dearest Mama and Dada,

This is especially for you today with all my thanks for helping me to become a better man and a better artist than I could ever have been without your guidance, encouragement and support. And without the wonderful upbringing you gave us all. It is worth more than riches and it can be passed down to my own children. If you are proud of me at times like this, then remember I am *always* proud of you.

All my love

Abram

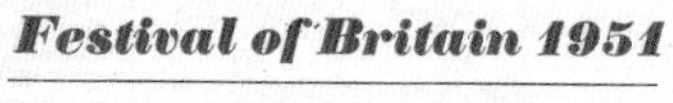
Festival of Britain 1951

2 SAVOY COURT LONDON WC2 — WATERLOO 1951

May 10, 1951

Dear Mr. Games,

Very many thanks indeed for sending me the signed Festival postage stamps, which I am happy to have and to keep as a souvenir of the Festival. I much appreciate your kind thought in sending them, and your good wishes.

Yours sincerely,

Gerald Barry

Gerald Barry
Director-General

Abram Games Esq., F.S.I.A.,
41 The Vale,
London,
N.W.11.

You must feel proud when you see the Symbol everywhere!

A letter to Abram from Gerald Barry, Director-General, Festival of Britain

Unofficial First Day Cover, 3rd May 1951, produced by HE Wingfield

Festival Boudicca envelope issued by the Philatelic Traders' Society and the British Philatelic Association, with a Festival machine cancellation

Souvenir albums of ten 3d blue, green, red, plum and black stamps, were sold in aid of the Greater London Fund for the Blind for two shillings and six pence. Separate sheets of ten stamps in the five colours were also available.

Abram's rejected stamp design rough to commemorate the death of Winston Churchill, 1965

'Souvenir Card' of Festival Commemorative Stamps printed for the Postmaster General

OFFICIAL GUIDE COVERS

On 4th September 1950, Abram received a contract from the Festival of Britain office to design eight official guide covers. He was to be awarded a fee of £215 5s 0d to cover the following schedule of work:

1. *Finished artwork of the basic cover design and the back cover.*
2. *Background colour guides.*
3. *Hand lettering for sub-titles.*
4. *Consultations with printers and typographer.*
5. *Use of design if used for advertising purposes.*

Abram was not yet experienced in the design of book jackets or catalogue covers. But he had produced a few in the 1930s and, whilst he was working in the War Office, he had designed the cover for the booklet 'Roof over Britain', two *Art and Industry* covers, two book jackets, a series of twelve covers for 'Target for Tomorrow' published by Pilot Books, and a few for *Future* magazine and other trade catalogues.

On the recommendation of Francis Meynell, Typographic Advisor to HMSO, Will Carter designed the inside layout and typography of the guides. He worked closely with Ian Cox, the Director of Science and Technology for the Festival, who was responsible for the content of all but the Science guide. The main page headings were in Rockwell Extra Bold and Times New Roman was the chosen body text. The Festival Office and the Publicity Planning Group encouraged successful companies, manufacturers and services to advertise in them. Although the advertising rates were expensive in comparison with magazine tariffs of the time, many businesses bought full colour advertisement space, as they were aware of the vast circulation of the guides and the benefits of being associated with the Festival. Fosh & Cross Ltd, London, printed the covers, except for the cover of the South Bank catalogue which Purnell and Sons printed. Three and a half million catalogues were produced, with the profits going to the Treasury. Almost one million copies of the South Bank guide were sold.

1951 view of the Dome of Discovery on the South Bank, seen from Waterloo Station

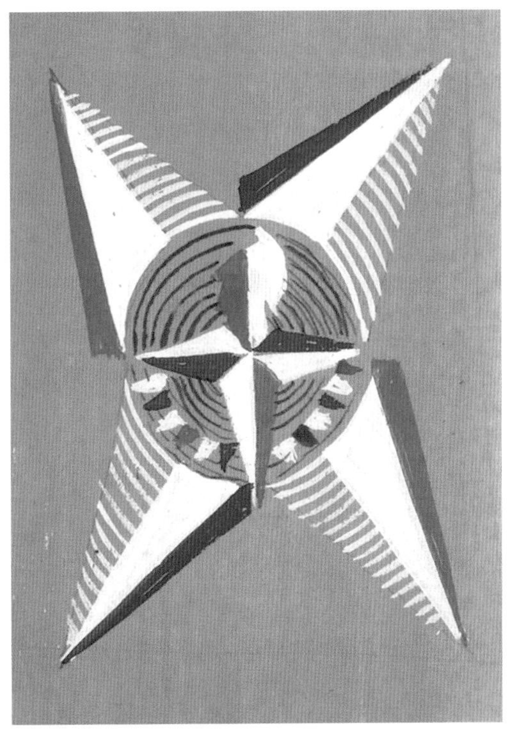

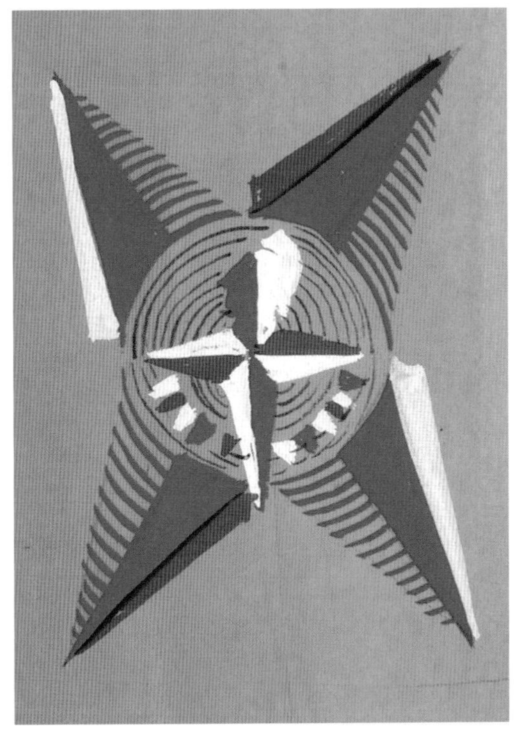

Preliminary rough sketches for the official guide covers

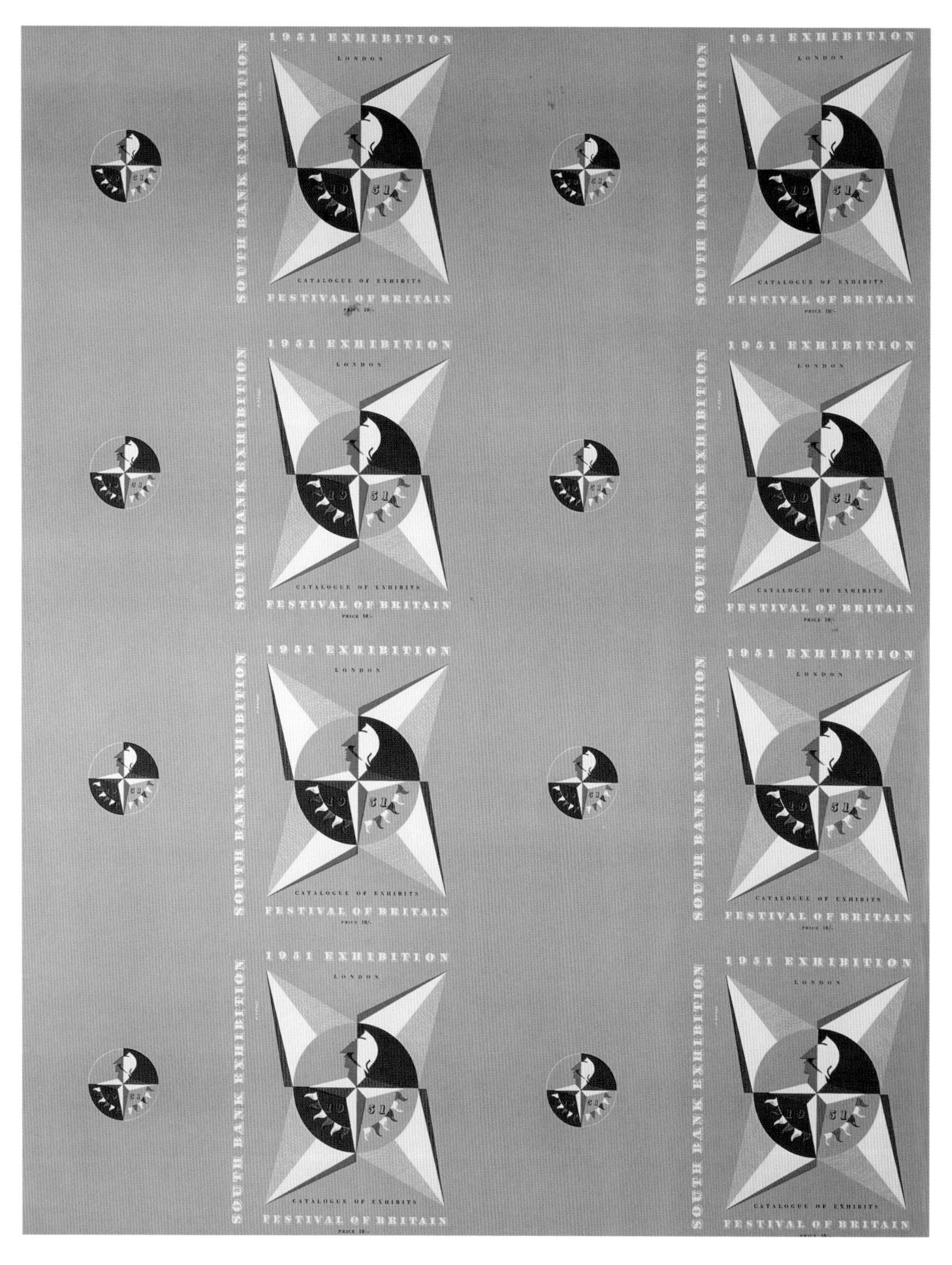

Untrimmed proof for the Catalogue of Exhibits

A Catalogue of Exhibits on show at the South Bank Exhibition was sold for ten shillings

1

This must have been a first rough design for the catalogue cover, as it has a title, but after second thoughts and probably not thinking it powerful enough, Abram moved the plain symbol in the circle to the back cover at a reduced size and added decoration to the image on the front cover as shown in the second design.

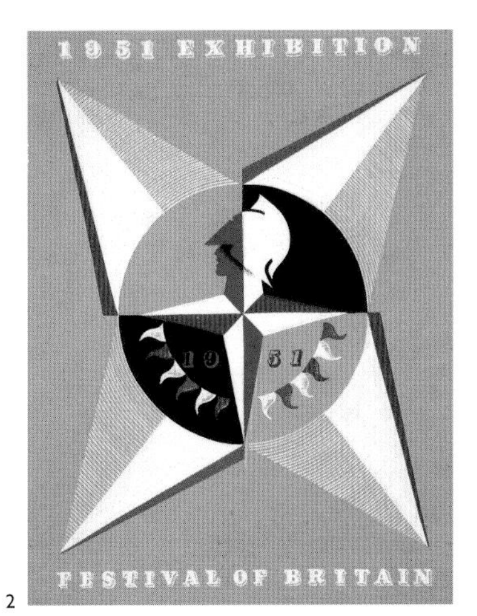

2

The first Festival cover Abram designed was for the South Bank Exhibition, London, which ran from 4th May to 30th September 1951. His Majesty's Stationery Office, published this 160 page official guide and the other seven. Two million copies were printed by Purnell & Sons Ltd and sold for two shillings and sixpence.

1, 2 and 3 are submission sketches

3

The Festival Ship, Campania, an aircraft carrier converted into a floating Festival exhibition, sailed to ten ports in Britain. From 4th May to 6th October, it travelled to Southampton, Dundee, Newcastle-upon-Tyne, Hull, Plymouth, Bristol, Cardiff, Belfast, Birkenhead and Glasgow. The price of the catalogue was two shillings.

The Ulster Farm & Factory Exhibition was held at Castlereagh, Belfast. The productive and craftsmanship skills of Northern Ireland's farms and factories were featured inside and outside a new factory on an industrial estate. The exhibition ran from 1st June to 31st August and the catalogue was sold for ninepence.

4

This catalogue was produced for the Land Travelling Exhibition, which although similar to the South Bank exhibition, highlighted industrial design. The world's largest travelling exhibition was taken by 100 lorries containing 40,000 square feet of 5,000 exhibits, to the industrial towns of Manchester, 5th to 26th May, Leeds, 23rd June to 14th July, Birmingham, 4th to 25th August and Nottingham, 15th September to 6th October. 100,000 copies were printed and it sold for two shillings.

5

Kelvin Hall in Glasgow, hosted an exhibition emphasizing the history and development of Britain's heavy engineering industry and concentrated on the importance of coal and water; the two main sources of power at the time. Shipbuilding, the railways and 'the power of the future' – atomic energy, were also represented. The exhibition, which opened 28th May was organized by Scottish Committee of the Festival Council and closed 18th August. The catalogue sold for two shillings.

6

The Exhibition of Science was held in the Science Museum in South Kensington on 4th May until 30th September. Over 150 British scientists contributed, including the new CoID Festival Pattern Group which was established to design textiles, wallpaper and products inspired by crystal structures, molecules and atoms. The catalogue, which was written by the scientist and science historian Dr Jacob Bronowski, was sold for two shillings.

4, 5, and 6 are submission sketches

Above: The rough and printed guide cover for the Exhibition of Architecture, Poplar

Left: Poster for the Lansbury Estate, Poplar, published by His Majesty's Stationery Office

The Exhibition of Architecture was held in Poplar, London, from 3rd May to 30th September 1951. It featured the new Lansbury Estate, commissioned by the London County Council and was built under the direction of Professor Patrick Abercrombie. The catalogue was priced at two shillings.

The Festival guides being sold at the Land Traveller exhibition

FESTIVAL FLAGS

Until 1948, James Holland was Chief Designer of Exhibitions and Display at the Central Office of Information. He became a principal designer for the Festival of Britain and supervised the Sea and Ships pavilion on the South Bank site. Responsible for the design of the Festival exhibition ship 'Campania', in October 1949, he suggested to the Presentation Panel that the Festival symbol should be adapted for use as a house flag. It was agreed that Abram Games was to be commissioned for this project. After a quick discussion, on 26th October, Abram went to Holland's office and without first discussing his fee, presented forty-five variations of his Festival symbol a few days later. This was to be the only flag Abram would design in his sixty-year-career.

Not only was the presentation of so many choices for approval out of character, but also Abram had 'jumped the gun'. A surprised Holland showed the roughs to Gerald Barry, the Presentation Panel and the Festival Design Group and all agreed that the designer 'had an excellent solution to the problem'. Abram then asked for a preliminary fee of forty guineas. Faced with a 'fait accompli', Holland had to consider if this was a reasonable sum. On 10th November he wrote to Abram to say that this was indeed acceptable and a further twenty-six guineas would be paid for final drawings and a basic flag manual. Abram replied on 17th November explaining that he hoped to carry out the job with a minimum of trouble and revision, but realized the difficulties of reaching a fast and clear decision. He related that the Festival Office had kept him in suspense for three agonizing months and if he seemed a little sensitive, Holland should understand. Abram, who never had patience for indecisiveness, received his official brief for the Festival Flag on 28th November 1949.

The brief for Abram was:

To consider the adaptation of the Festival symbol, which you designed, for use as a flag, banner or pennant for general Festival service and, in particular, as a house flag for the Festival Ship 'Campania'.

You are required to investigate this problem in relation to:

- a. *production of the flag.*
- b. *the heraldic limitations and traditions of flag design.*
- c. *the avoidance of any confusion or infringement of existing flag designs.*

Sketches showing your proposed designs, together with a report are to be submitted. It is suggested that although the symbol as a flag device must have a recognizable affinity with the original symbol, considerable simplification may be necessary to secure a striking design.

Unusually, Abram was also asked to prepare an alternative design, in 'sketch form' without extra fee, should his first design be unacceptable. This must have infuriated him as he was always so confident in his work and would only submit one design for consideration. He adapted his Festival Britannia, without including her head, as he was aware that a fluttering flag on a ship is difficult to read at long distance. The flag had to be simple and bold.

The Campania, built by Harland and Wolff in Belfast, in 1941, was a 16,000 ton Escort aircraft

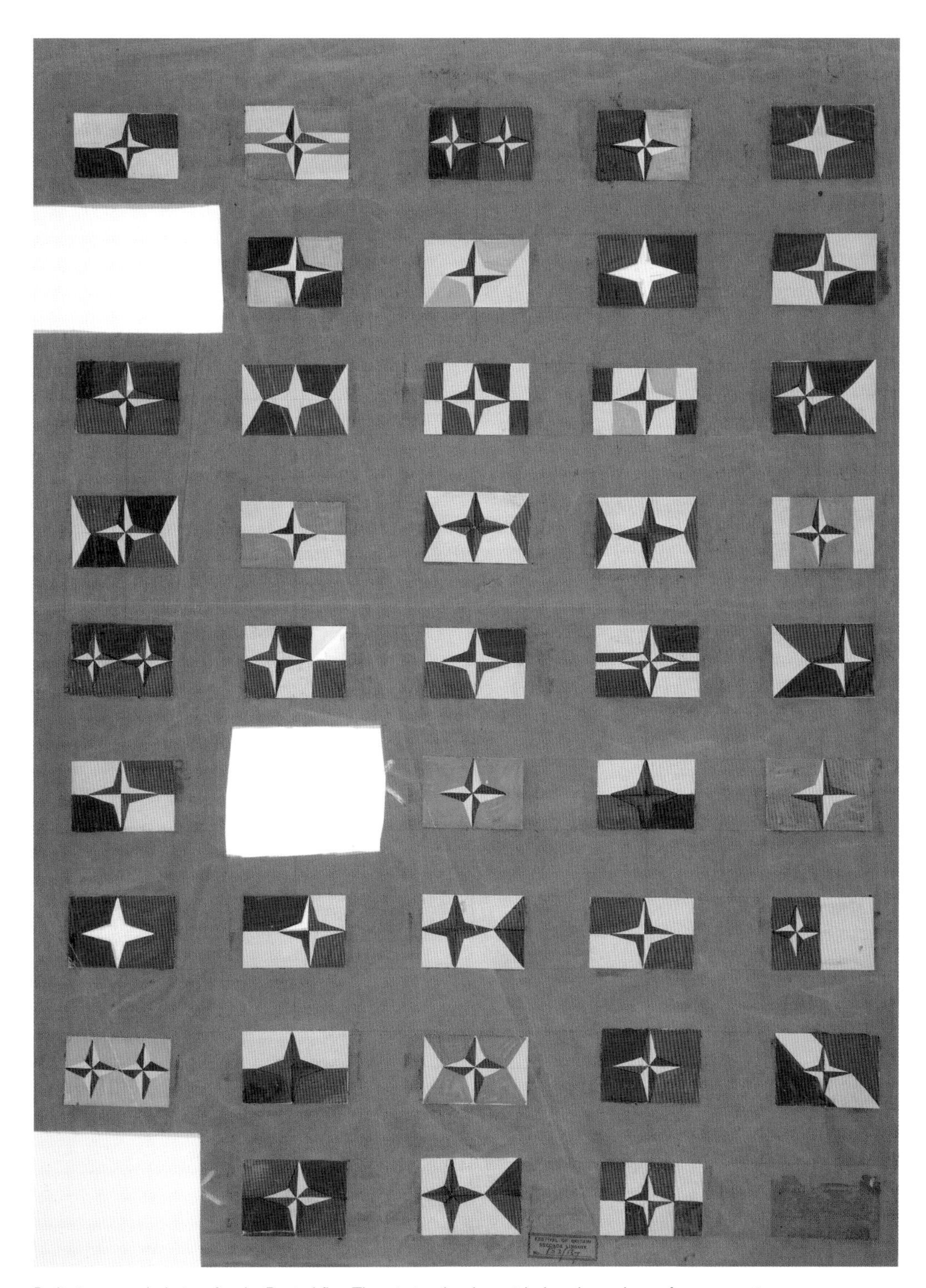

Preliminary rough designs for the Festival flag. The missing sketches might have been chosen for presentation

The Festival ship, Campania

carrier on loan from the Admiralty. She was painted white and transformed into a floating exhibition ship during the Festival of Britain, touring major British ports and Belfast. After the Festival, she was re-commissioned for service and carried the equipment for the British Atomic weapon testing on Montebello Island, North West Australia. Returning first to Chatham and then to Blyth in Northumberland, the Campania was decommissioned in 1955.

Abram wrote a flag guide:

THE DESIGN AND USE OF FESTIVAL FLAGS

During 1951 the Festival of Britain flags should be in evidence not only at the official exhibition sites, but also throughout the country, wherever local authorities have planned their own Festival celebrations.

Festival flags have been designed by Mr Abram Games FSIA (Fellow of the Society of Industrial Artists), who is also the designer of the Festival symbol, which appears as the device on the flags.

Rather than adopt a single flag, the Festival organizers have accepted a design that can be worked out in three different colour arrangements. One consists of a blue and white star on a red ground, one of a blue and red star on a white ground, and one of a red and white star on a blue ground. The decorative possibilities of grouping such flags are considerably wider than if one colour scheme only had been approved. There is no intention of allotting any one of these flags for an exclusive purpose, but the red and blue star on a white ground will be used as house flag on the Festival Ship, 'Campania'.

It is felt very strongly that, while the widest use of the flags is encouraged, it is important that the quality of the flags themselves is first-class. The flags, as well as being decorations, are to be treated as exhibits, and should be evidence of British achievement in this particular field. In particular, the precise character and tone of the selected colours must be employed and the proportion of the star be maintained. THE FLAGS ARE NOT JUST RED, WHITE AND BLUE. *They are particular shades and tones of these colours, and the balance between the red and blue must not be lost, if the flags are to retain their character. For the guidance of contractors who may be making flags for use during Festival year, the Festival Office has prepared the attached specification and colour samples:*

The flags should be in proportion of 3:2, and can be of any size. For special purposes, eg. Venetian banners, etc, other shapes may be necessary, but there should be no attempt to vary the proportion of the star device to fit these shapes, and the design should depend on the placing of the device on the field.

Of course, the flags had their critics. *The Truth* wondered why it was necessary that the Festival have its own flag. Was the Union Jack not good enough for Gerald Barry?

Thirty-two years later, in 1983, Abram oversaw the manufacture of a new flag, based on his Festival symbol, for the South Bank's Festival Pier. Originally sited at Battersea Pleasure Gardens, the pier was relocated. This was the idea of Tony Banks, Chairman of the Greater London's Council's Arts and Recreation Committee. It was built on the remains of a 1951 Festival pontoon and a wartime-unexploded bomb was dredged up from the Thames during its construction.

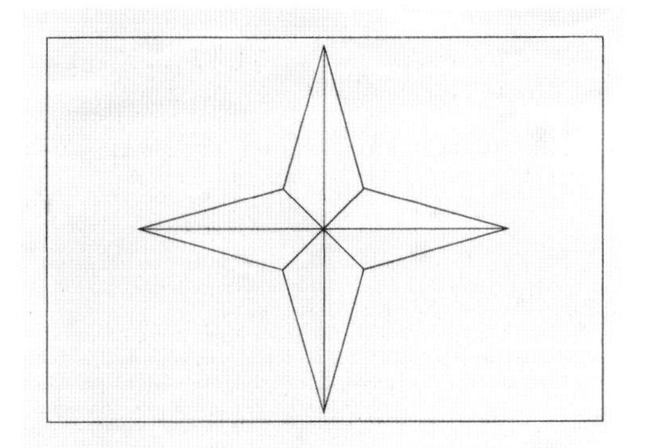

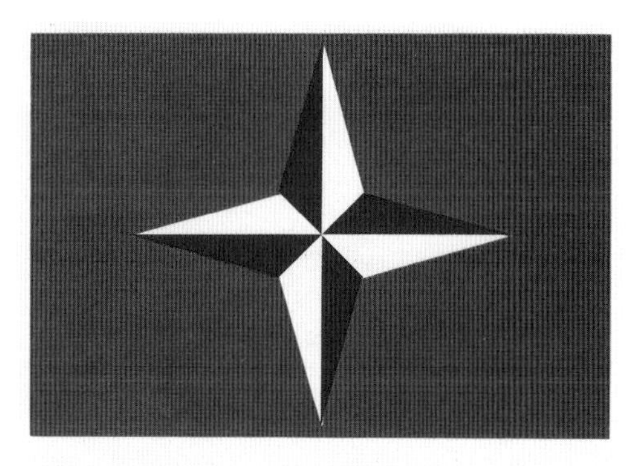

Above: Key drawing for all flags showing proportions and position of the star
Below: The design to be used as House Flag on the Festival Ship "Campania"

Above and below: The alternative designs on coloured grounds. It is very important that these colours be strictly adhered to.

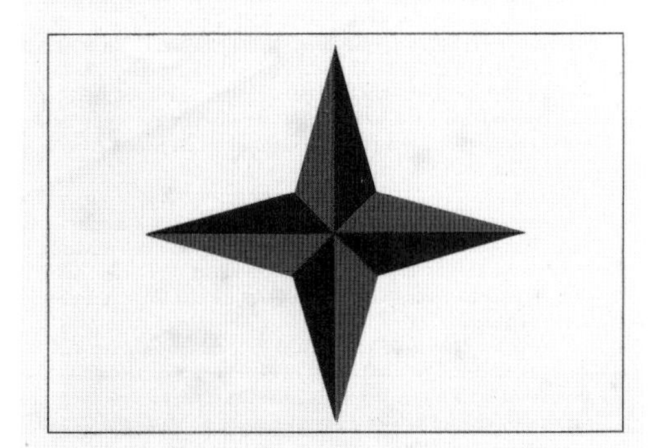

The Flag manual

The Festival symbol on the Campania

During the run of the Festival, a forty-foot high Festival 'Star', weighing over a ton, hung in Northumberland Avenue. Made from magnesium alloy, it was an ambitious structure and led visitors onto a temporary Bailey bridge, which linked the north, and south of the river, into the South Bank site. It was floodlit by night. Jack Howe was responsible for the Festival decorations and illuminations.

The Festival flags on the Bailey bridge

The shipbuilding section of the Sea and Ships pavilion, South Bank, London. The star is on the ventilation funnel.

The Festival flag and stars hung along York Road, South Bank, London. Architects' Co-operative Partnership designed the screen.

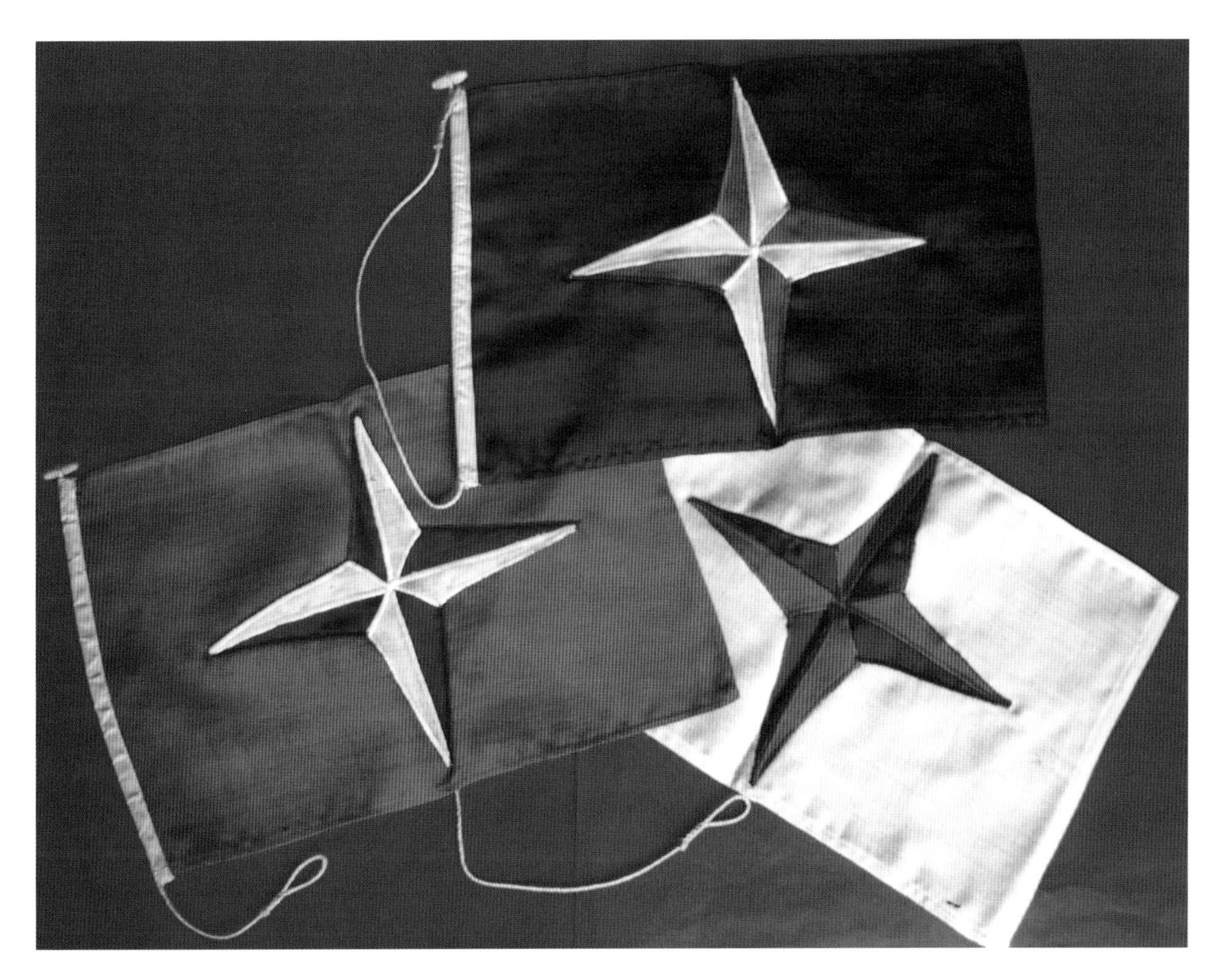

The three colour ways of the Festival flags

The Festival flag on the Festival pier, South Bank, London, 1991

SOUTH BANK PLAN GUIDES

The Festival of Britain Office instructed Abram to deliver his design for the Festival plan by 28th February 1951. On 20th March 1951, he received a cheque for £52 and ten shillings for the final artwork, which he was allowed to sign. As with other Festival publicity, Abram had no hand in the design or content of the inside of the folder. It is not known who drew the inside map of the South Bank site. The double-fold Plan Guide was in a format suitable to be put in a pocket and easily posted. It was printed for HMSO by Fosh and Cross Ltd and sold for 3d.

Progressive sketches for plan

An unused design for the South Bank plan

Wiseman's National Savings Committee cover was printed by Fosh and Cross Ltd and is similar to Abram's first, unused design

South Bank plan, printed for HMSO by Fosh and Cross Ltd

Although similar in format, these programmes were not designed by Abram

Battersea Park guide

Festival programme folder designed by the London Press Agency, printed for HMSO by Waterlow and Sons Ltd

'FLOW OF COMMERCE' CHART

George Grenfell-Baines and Heinz J. Reifenberg designed the Power and Production Pavilion on the South Bank. It boasted a fifty foot viewing window made from the largest plate glass sheet in the world, which was manufactured by Pilkington Brothers.

The commission from the Festival of Britain Office to design a decorative chart for the pavilion came on 24th August 1950 with instructions to present preliminary designs by 30th September. It was to measure 33 feet by 5 feet 6 inches and its theme was to be 'Commerce'.

Abram, who had some experience designing murals and flow charts for the War Office and for various publications, informed the committee what his charges would be. They, however, were unhappy with his suggested fee. He explained to the Festival Committee that the work would be complicated in both design and

execution and he would require an assistant to 'climb step ladders'. Should the mural be in three dimensions, his price would be more. After several exchanges of memos, Gerald Barry agreed that 'Mr Games was the only artist in the country who could carry out the work' and he should be paid the fee he quoted; £315. Abram was asked to submit preliminary designs for which he would be paid £78.15.0d. The work had to be executed in full colour and to scale. He was to supervise the fixing and installation of the mural on site in the pavilion and he was also to maintain the work during the run of the exhibition.

Winter 1950 was a hectic time in the Games household. Abram, busier than ever, still taught one day a week at the Royal College of Art, and his two small children were running around the studio at home. If he was to meet the tight deadline, he needed an assistant, so he searched amongst his students at the college. At first a young man was employed, but he proved unsuitable for the job. Mona Caller was a perfect replacement. Not only did she work to Abram's high standards, she baby-sat the children and became a lifelong friend to the family. The mural filled the ground floor of the house, from the studio at the back, through the French windows into the living room. Abram considered it vital to view his work at a distance but Mona recalls that the panels of the mural were far too large for the space. From the wrong end of a telescope, Abram studied his design, thus reducing the proportions and enabling him to visualize how it would appear when complete. Marianne, Abram's wife, was a talented textile designer and often helped out in the studio. Abram would send her up the ladders to paint or touch up the mural, whilst she was pregnant, with me, their third child. Although Mona remembers working from clear working drawings, no records of these or final artwork can be traced. The mural was placed at high level in the 'Machines at Work' section in the Power and Production Pavilion. Hugh Casson judged Abram's mural one of the best at the Festival, even though it did not feature the symbol.

POSTERS

Although Abram designed the Festival symbol, the Festival Committee never asked him to design posters. However, being free of copyright, Britannia was used by many other designers on their posters and, as with the souvenirs, Abram was never consulted nor his opinion sought.

This official poster used Abram's artwork and the main text was made up from the official display Festival alphabet. Philip Boydell was a British designer and typographer, working for the London Press Exchange. The Planning and Publicity Group and the Festival's Press Office commissioned Boydell's 'Festival Titling' in 1949. The Festival of Britain's Typography Panel was set up soon afterwards, mainly in reaction to the unanimous dislike of the type. It was too late to amend and Abram, whilst acknowledging that it might reflect his symbol, thought it weak, characterless and inconsistent. In March 1951, the Architectural Review agreed. They thought it 'mean in conception and completely undistinguished in form'. The typeface appeared on posters, Festival leaflets, catalogues, booklets and advertisements, though was rarely used after 1951.

ABCDEFGHIJKLMNOP
QRSTUVWXYZ&ÆŒ

Monotype Festival Titling 554
designed by Phillip Boydell

A prestige Festival poster for home consumption designed by the London Press Agency and printed for HMSO by WS Cowell Ltd

To ensure a high standard in the design of the posters displayed in the vicinity of the South Bank exhibition, the Festival organisers arranged a poster competition. British advertisers and popular British advertising agencies were invited to enter new and never before seen posters. Winners would have their 16-sheet posters displayed on 15 large sites in York Road facing the South Bank. Only 67 posters, most of them specially commissioned for the competition, were submitted and 15 winners were chosen. Having designed another poster for them in 1949, Abram was commissioned by Murphy Radio, through the CR Casson Advertising Agency, to design a poster showing how television could be enjoyed in the home. He designed the poster in 1950 and his was the first to be chosen and hung on the hoardings.

The judges claimed that the standards of the entries were not as high as they had hoped for. In 1952 Abram expressed regret that having gained a showing, many of the successful advertisers slid back into their 'normal poster routine', their standards dropping. He urged both advertisers and artists to remember their responsibilities and complained that due to the public's receptive mood after the Festival, it would be easy to get away with 'a sea of rubbish' and harder to pioneer new paths.

Festival poster, designer unknown. It was also used as a card for the Festival Office.

Festival, Exhibition of Science poster by Robin Day for HMSO

Progressive sketches and final Murphy Television poster, 1949

The Society of Industrial Artists, the Council of Industrial Design and the British Federation of Master Printers, organized the first open-air International Poster Exhibition. Two hundred and fifty posters, from 17 countries on both sides of the Iron Curtain, were displayed from 30th June to 28th July 1951 in Victoria Embankment Gardens, London. Abram was one of five who selected the works on show. His poster for the Household Cavalry was placed between a poster from America and one from Russia.

Commercial art students were invited from London County Council's art schools to design the poster, that would advertise the International Poster Exhibition. Again, Abram was one of the five judges, including Ashley Haviden and FHK Henrion, who awarded a total of fifty guineas prize money.

Cecil Cooke, Director of Festival of Britain Exhibitions, and Abram, judged another competition inviting schoolgirls to design a poster, which would convey the concept of the Festival. The prizes totalled £40 and the posters were exhibited at the New Horticultural Hall, Westminster from 24th May to 3rd June 1951.

Progressive sketches for the Murphy Television poster, 1950

Pasting the Murphy poster on the South Bank site

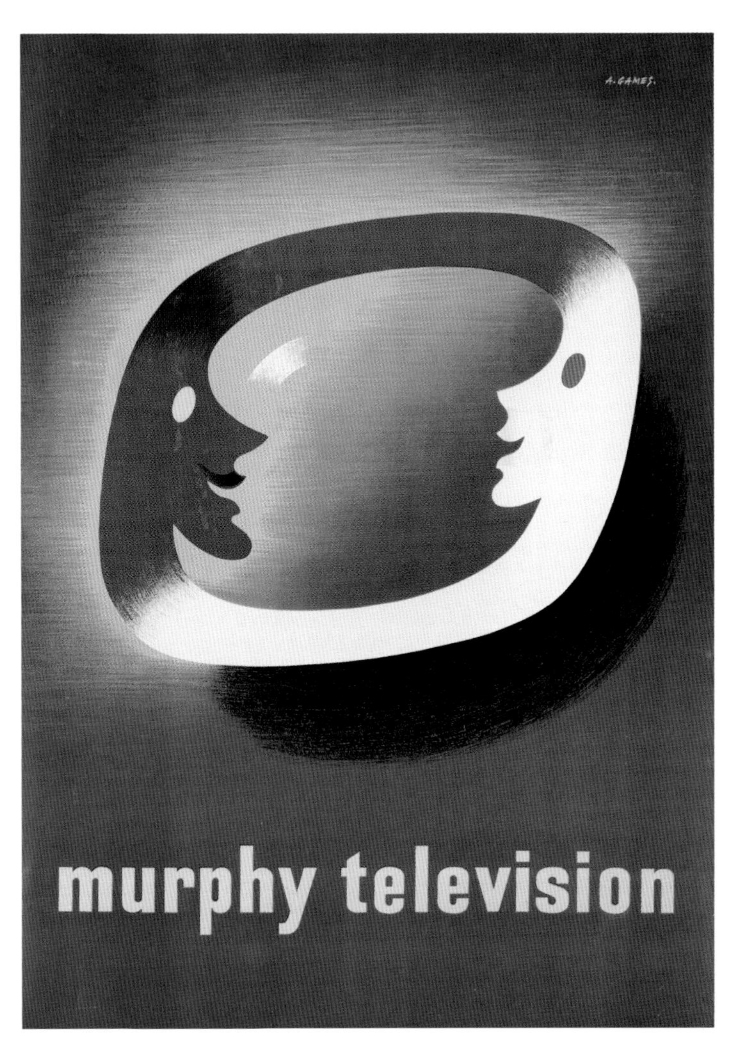

Murphy Television poster, 1950

The Festival construction begins, the York Road poster hoarding is on the right

This 1951 London Transport poster was used in Underground trains and buses going to the South Bank. Festival information was added beneath the poster. Central London Underground Stations also had special decoration to celebrate the Festival as shown left.

In 1950, Abram was commissioned by the British Overseas Aircraft Corporation and London Transport to create Festival posters. He ingeniously referred to several elements of his symbol without including it in the posters.

The 'Model Engineer Exhibition', organized by Percy Marshall and Co Ltd, publishers of magazines for model makers, was held during the Festival at the New Horticultural Hall, London between 22nd August and 1st September 1951. Abram designed this poster.

Recruitment poster,
1949

RELIEF MODEL OF THE SYMBOL

On 3rd January 1951 the Festival Office sent Abram this 'Schedule of Work'.

1. *To advise on the preparation of a plaster replica of the Festival of Britain symbol.*
2. *To undertake such modelling of the head of the symbol as may be required to enable the Display Contractor to obtain the true representation.*
3. *To supervise the manufacture by Art Plastics Ltd of the plaster replica.*

This work had to be completed by 14th February 1951 and a fee of £52 10s 0d, to cover all related work, was agreed. He interpreted his design for the sculptured relief out of plaster and it was to be used for many venues over Britain.

Abram made this plaque from plaster

In 1953, Abram was passing the Savoy Court Festival offices in London and, noticing that the building was being converted, he asked the builders where the Festival shield was. 'Don't know mate, try the skip.' came the response. And there it was! It had been displayed outside the office from 1948 to 1951.

Award of Merit plaque made by Poole Pottery, Dorset, still outside White City Underground station, London

Right: David Trussler designed the Festival plaques on 219 Oxford Street, London. Ronald Ward and Partners designed the building, built by August 1951, for the boxing promoter, Jack Solomons.

H Wilson Parker working on his design for the 'Award of Merit' plaque. The award was given by the Council of Architecture for good design in building and landscaping in 1951.

Abram in his studio with the Festival plaster plaque on the wall, 1957

FESTIVAL SOUVENIRS AND CURIOS

Not only did Abram collect Festival items, he proudly kept a large 'scrap book' of Festival ephemera, letters and photographs. The album was bound and the Festival emblem embossed on the cover by Peter Waters, a student of Abram's, and Roger Powell, the bookbinding tutor from the Royal College of Art. Both Waters and Powell were highly respected and became the twentieth century's most influential bookbinders.

The copyright-free Festival emblem appeared in various guises, many to Abram's amusement. The emblem was baked into loaves of bread, it was stencilled onto taxis, printed on powder compacts, sown into flower-beds, woven into rugs and camisole knickers, embossed into chocolate, biscuits and bars of soap, and even appeared on a rat trap. Souvenir badges were prevalent. In 1951, the press reported that unless the Ministry of Supply allowed the use of non-ferrous metals, which had been banned due to the war, few badges could be manufactured. The Festival of Britain Souvenir Committee kept a keen eye on the souvenirs and would not allow foreign or unofficial souvenirs, many made from scrapped war aeroplanes, to be sold on the South Bank.

Part of a leaflet for a Festival rat trap

The souvenir which Abram cherished most was a photograph. His closest school friends became medical practitioners and one day he was invited to meet them at a London hospital, but was urged to keep the visit secret. The friends took him to the hospital's histological laboratory. One of the friends had removed 604 gallstones, which had contributed to the death of one patient, and the doctors had irreverently rearranged them. Abram was flabbergasted at the one-foot tall emblem, which was laid in front of him.

604 gallstones

A commemorative wall hanging in the Festival Trinity Methodist Church, Poplar, London

One of six rainwater hopper-heads on the Lansbury Estate, Poplar, London

Council street sign in Clapham, London

A Festival clock, designed by Robert Elden Minns, on the wall of a Steel Finishing Works in Derbyshire. The figures spell 'ANAVIO', the name of the Roman fort at Brough. Hence the clock hands representing a Roman eagle and fasces (a bundle of wooden sticks and axe blade).

The Festival emblem made from flowers

A Festival of Britain door-plate, the location is unknown

Stencil plate for Hackney carriages

Michael Hymers, a Festival collector, made this stained-glass pane for an interior door in his home

A Rowntree Fruit Gums box

Festival of Britain bread

A Huntley and Palmers Festival biscuit

A Nestlé Festival chocolate wrapper

A Nestlé Festival chocolate coin

One of many designs for Festival powder compacts

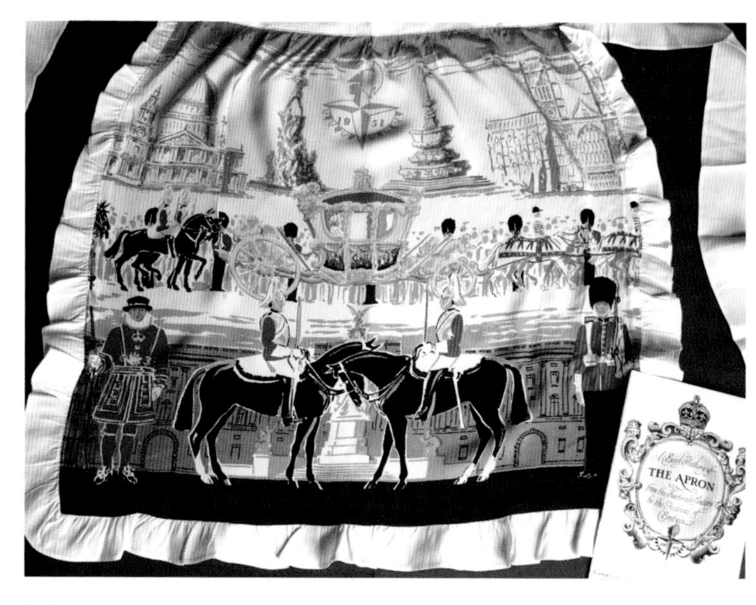

A Festival of Britain apron

Festival soap

A still wearable machine-knitted Festival woollen jumper made by I and R Morley Ltd. There was also a Paton and Baldwins hand-knit jumper pattern available.

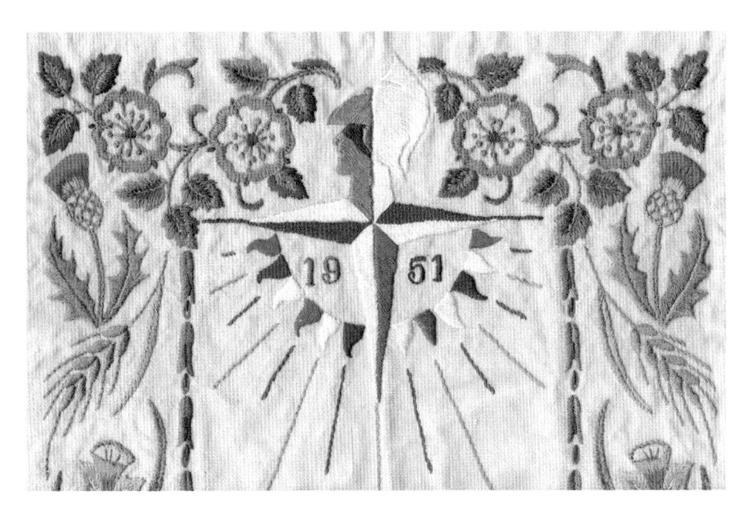

Details from two of the many commemorative Festival embroidery kits

There were many scarves designed for the Festival. These are made from silk crepe-de-chine.

Die-cut ‘Dancing Britannia’ by George Adams-Teltscher

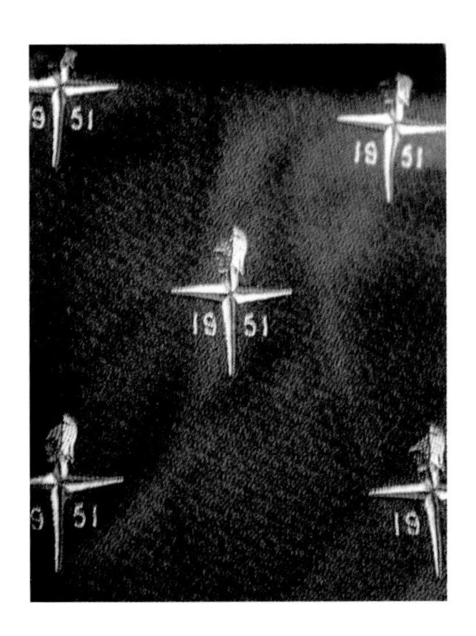

A detail from a tie worn by staff at the South Bank site, made by Darenth Fabric Printing Company Ltd

Badges and an armband worn by staff at the South Bank site

Festival passes. The identities of the holders are unknown

A Festival London Transport bus ticket

A leaflet for Raleigh Industries Ltd

A Festival Skylon Biro souvenir desk pen and holder designed by Willy M de Majo for the Miles-Martin Pen Company. It was sold by Richard Pye and Company Ltd at 25 shillings.

Three of the many Festival souvenir badges, a commemorative key ring and a tie pin

One of a pair of wooden plaques made in 1951 by scientific engineers, RW Munro Ltd, for its factory display. Munro supplied the wind vane for the top of the Skylon.

Right: Abram's drawing of his Cona Rex coffee maker. Although not yet in full production, a prototype Cona Rex was displayed in the Breakfast Bar, Kitchen with Living Room section of the Homes and Gardens Pavilion on the South Bank. Having designed a beautiful sculpture with both form and function, Abram's coffee percolator was eventually manufactured in 1952 from aluminium from recycled Spitfires. As the coffee grains and boiling water never come into contact with metal, this coffee maker creates excellent coffee. He redesigned the Cona in 1962.

One of many Festival paperweights made in what was termed three-dimensional plastic by Wilmot Breedon

Right: Oscar's Festival Café, Oscar Road, Broadstairs, Kent, 2010

Proud son, Brian Powney, wearing a Festival costume and holding a shield, both made by his father, 1951

The 60th birthday cake for George Simner, a founder member of the Festival of Britain Society

When George died in 2008, his family and the Society contributed to this floral Festival wreath as a fitting tribute to him

TELEKINEMA

To publicize Britain's contribution to the film industry, the Festival Committee and the British Film Institute established a Telekinema (or Telecinema) and Television Pavilion on the South Bank site. Industrial documentaries produced by private industry, films demonstrating latest techniques such as stereoscopy and binaural sound, and short cultural and scientific films relating to the Festival of Britain were shown there. Designed by the Canadian architect Wells Wintemute Coates, who was also responsible for its interior, the modern, 400-seat cinema, screened both film and large-screen television for the first time in the world. It was in this cinema that many people first experienced television and where they excitedly donned special 3D glasses to watch four new stereoscopic 35mm films. In 1957, the Telekinema was pulled down and replaced by the National Film Theatre.

Thelma Cazalet-Kier was on the Board of Directors of the Festival Film Productions with Sir Kenneth Clark and Sir Stephen Tallents. No love was lost between Cazalet-Kier and Abram, as she was instrumental in banning his ATS 'Blonde Bombshell' recruiting poster in 1942. However, Abram had a high regard for Tallents, who commissioned him years earlier to design posters for the Post Office.

Not only did Abram design the fire curtain for the cinema, but his symbol was also used in the film titles for Family Portrait, directed by Humphrey Jennings in 1950, and the Magic Box directed by John Boulting in 1951.

FESTIVAL CARTOONS AND ADAPTATIONS

Buying a birthday or Christmas card was always discouraged in the Games household. Abram expected his children to design their own cards. After all, he spent precious hours making friends and family custom made cards for special occasions. The Games's Christmas card in 1951 starred Britannia as the Christmas tree fairy.

Fougasse, also known as Cyril Kenneth Bird, designed the cover of *Punch* for April 1951. Presenting a copy to Abram, he wrote on it, 'to Abram Games, this is sincerest flattery.' He enclosed a letter; 'Herewith, with much admiration for the original design, a base travesty'. Abram appreciated that the cartoonists who lampooned many of his designs throughout his career recognized his work. The Festival emblem was no exception. The advertising agencies had fun with the symbol also.

Birthday card for grandpa by Theo aged 9, 1996

'Never mind what I remind you of, George – take this line and tie it to the broken piece.' Ronald Niebour (NEB)

The Games family's Christmas card, 1950

In 1979 Professor Richard Guyatt, then Rector at the Royal College of Art, designed a poster advertising a lecture Sir Hugh Casson was to give on the Festival of Britain. Both Guyatt and Casson, the Director of Architecture for the Festival, were Abram's good friends.

Festival Director, Exhibitions and Deputy Chairman, Cecil Cooke's Christmas card, 1950

Far left: Cover for The Tatler, 9th May 1951, artist unknown

Left: Cover for Punch by Cyril Bird (Fougasse)

Below: Plymouth communist party featured Stalin instead of Britannia on their Festival programme

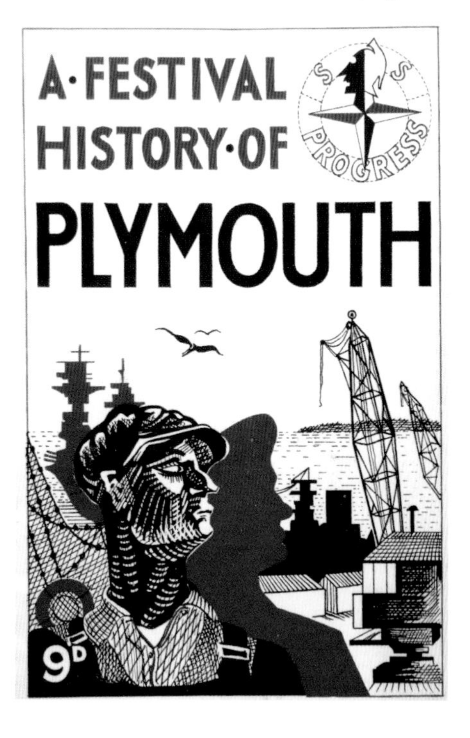

The advertising agencies had fun with the Festival symbol

Festival souvenir and event programmes

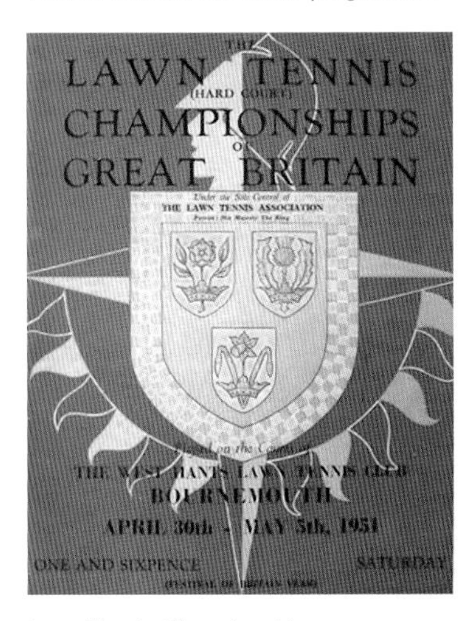

Lawn Tennis Championships

Nottingham

Poole

Southampton

'Our Town' Walthamstow

Lansbury Estate, Polar

Wolverhampton symbol with the crossed keys of St Peter over-layed

Norwich

London Society of Magicians

City of Cardiff

Metropolitan Borough of Camberwell

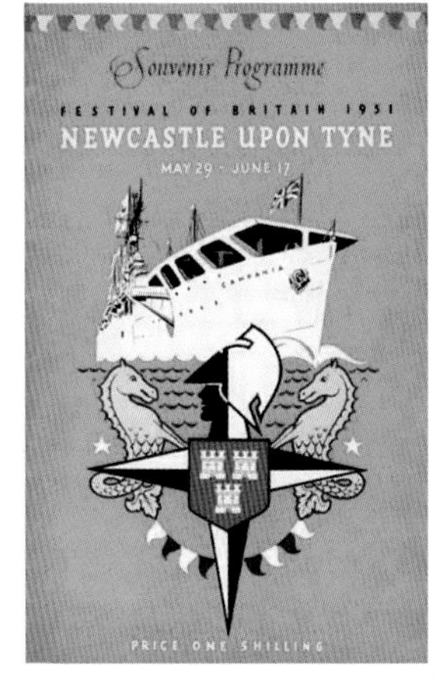

Newcastle upon Tyne

Portsmouth and Southsea

Daily Mail 21st March 1951, by Illingworth

News Chronicle 1951, the Festive Round by Roy Ullyett

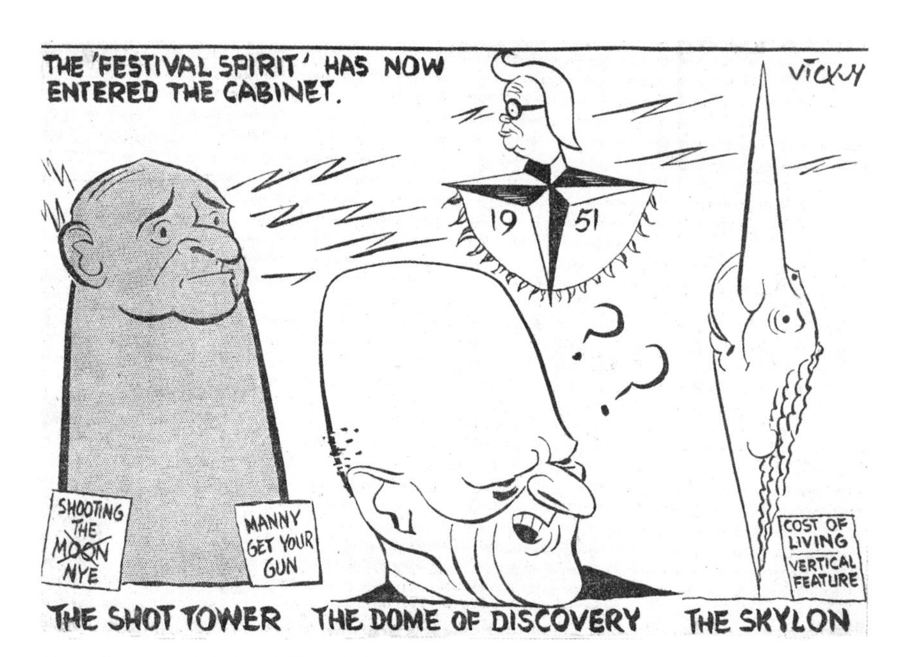

News Chronicle, 30th May 1951, by Vicky

Cartoonist unknown but possibly Roy Ullyett, 1951

Vicky's Festival Fantasia, News Chronicle 5th May 1951

By Horrabin

A detail from a cartoon by Joseph Lee, Evening News 2nd May 1951

Star 28th April 1951, by Joss

By Biro

By Moon

Newspaper heading, Irish Independent, 14th April 1951

A detail from the cover of 'Imagery'

Concert programme

Festival advert

"Curtain's just going up, Miss." cartoonist unknown

In 1991, the Royal Designers for Industry gave a dinner for faculty members to commemorate the 40th anniversary of the Festival of Britain. Many of its designers and architects were still alive and came to celebrate. Abram was asked to design the cover for the menu. Although Margaret Thatcher had resigned as Prime Minister of the United Kingdom six months earlier, she had left an eleven-year legacy, so he turned Britannia into Thatcher, complete with handbag and hands on hips.

Birthday card for Abram by daughter Naomi, 1991

News Chronicle 26th April 1951, by Vicky

"Steady now, boys and girls....here come the critics!"
Evening News 4th May 1951, by Joseph Lee

"Wait for it! No souvenirs 'till Sunday, when the place will be officially closed."
Evening News 2nd September 1951, by Joseph Lee

ROYAL FESTIVAL HALL 40TH ANNIVERSARY POSTER

Abram was delighted when he was asked to design the poster to celebrate the fortieth anniversary of the Royal Festival Hall in 1991. The building, designed by Leslie Martin, Robert Matthews and Peter Moro, from the London County Council's Architects' Department, was the first public building to be constructed in London after the war. Having taken three years to design and build, it was opened at the start of the Festival of Britain and is the only building on the South Bank left as a reminder of 1951. The poster was silkscreen printed by G & B Arts.

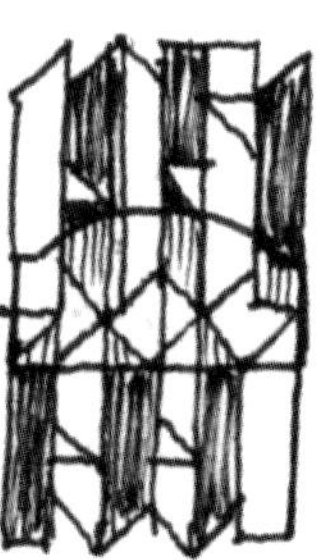

Progressive sketches for the anniversary poster

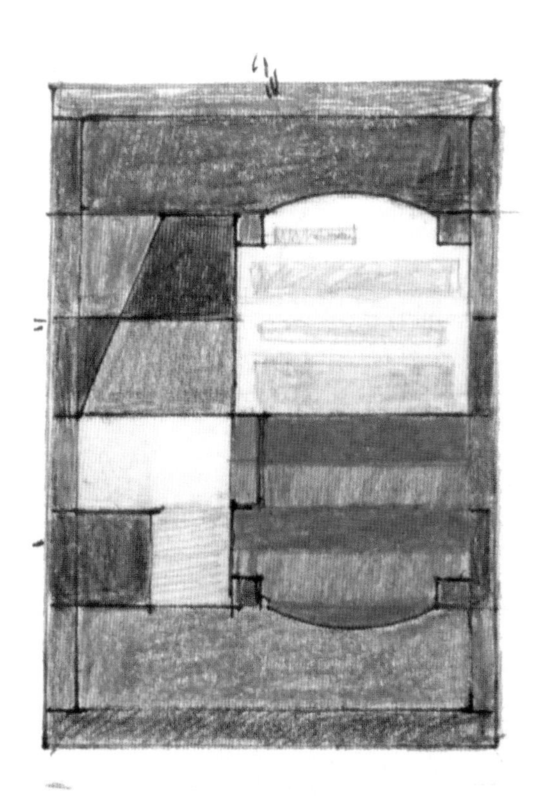

Abram is now sure of his final design

Fortieth anniversary poster for the Royal Festival Hall, London, 1991

CONCLUSION

During the five Festival months in 1951, the festivities in London were attended by 8.5 million visitors and millions more enjoyed the festivities all over the United Kingdom. No-one ever forgot the experience. The Festival provoked much controversy, especially as it cost £8 million, but post-war drab Britain was now alive with dazzling colour and optimism.

The Festival style was to have a lasting effect on Britain and inspire many young architects and designers. Although all trace of the South Bank site was soon to be obliterated by Winston Churchill and his new Conservative government, the Festival of Britain was considered a huge success and Abram was proud to be a part of it.

On the occasion of the First Visit of Their Majesties the King and Queen

The Chairman and Council of
THE FESTIVAL OF BRITAIN
are desired by His Majesty's Government to request
the honour of the Company of

Mr. Abram Games and one guest.

at the South Bank Exhibition, London
on Friday, May 4, 1951, at 11 a.m.

Lounge Suit

R. S. V. P. The Ceremonial Officer
2 Savoy Court, London, W.C.2